William Shakespeare

THE MERCHANT
OF VENICE

Edited with a Commentary by W. Moelwyn Merchant
Introduced by Peter Holland

PENGUIN BOOKS

PENGUIN BOOKS

Published by the Penguin Group
Penguin Books Ltd, 80 Strand, London WC2R ORL, England
Penguin Group (USA) Inc., 375 Hudson Street, New York, New York 10014, USA
Penguin Group (Canada), 10 Alcorn Avenue, Toronto, Ontario, Canada M4V 3B2
(a division of Pearson Penguin Canada Inc.)
Penguin Ireland, 25 St Stephen's Green, Dublin 2, Ireland (a division of Penguin Books Ltd)
Penguin Group (Australia), 250 Camberwell Road, Camberwell, Victoria 3124, Australia
(a division of Pearson Australia Group Pty Ltd)
Penguin Books India Pvt Ltd, 11 Community Centre, Panchsheel Park, New Delhi – 110 017, India
Penguin Group (NZ), cnr Airborne and Rosedale Roads, Albany, Auckland 1310, New Zealand
(a division of Pearson New Zealand Ltd)
Penguin Books (South Africa) (Pty) Ltd, 24 Sturdee Avenue, Rosebank 2196, South Africa

Penguin Books Ltd, Registered Offices: 80 Strand, London WC2R ORL, England

www.penguin.com

This edition fiirst published in Penguin Books 1967
Reissued in the Penguin Shakespeare series 2005

1

This edition copyright © Penguin Books, 1967
Account of the Text and Commentary copyright © W. Moelwyn Merchant, 1967
General Introduction and Chronology copyright © Stanley Wells, 2005
Introduction, The Play in Performance and Further Reading copyright © Peter Holland, 2005

The moral right of the editors has been asserted

Set in 11.5/12.5 PostScript Monotype Fournier
Typeset by Palimpsest Book Production Limited, Polmont, Stirlingshire
Printed in England by Clays Ltd, St Ives plc

Contents

General Introduction

Every play by Shakespeare is unique. This is part of his greatness. A restless and indefatigable experimenter, he moved with a rare amalgamation of artistic integrity and dedicated professionalism from one kind of drama to another. Never shackled by convention, he offered his actors the alternation between serious and comic modes from play to play, and often also within the plays themselves, that the repertory system within which he worked demanded, and which provided an invaluable stimulus to his imagination. Introductions to individual works in this series attempt to define their individuality. But there are common factors that underpin Shakespeare's career.

Nothing in his heredity offers clues to the origins of his genius. His upbringing in Stratford-upon-Avon, where he was born in 1564, was unexceptional. His mother, born Mary Arden, came from a prosperous farming family. Her father chose her as his executor over her eight sisters and his four stepchildren when she was only in her late teens, which suggests that she was of more than average practical ability. Her husband John, a glover, apparently unable to write, was nevertheless a capable businessman and loyal townsfellow, who seems to have fallen on relatively hard times in later life. He would have been brought up as a Catholic, and may have retained

Catholic sympathies, but his son subscribed publicly to Anglicanism throughout his life.

The most important formative influence on Shakespeare was his school. As the son of an alderman who became bailiff (or mayor) in 1568, he had the right to attend the town's grammar school. Here he would have received an education grounded in classical rhetoric and oratory, studying authors such as Ovid, Cicero and Quintilian, and would have been required to read, speak, write and even think in Latin from his early years. This classical education permeates Shakespeare's work from the beginning to the end of his career. It is apparent in the self-conscious classicism of plays of the early 1590s such as the tragedy of *Titus Andronicus*, *The Comedy of Errors*, and the narrative poems *Venus and Adonis* (1592–3) and *The Rape of Lucrece* (1593–4), and is still evident in his latest plays, informing the dream visions of *Pericles* and *Cymbeline* and the masque in *The Tempest*, written between 1607 and 1611. It inflects his literary style throughout his career. In his earliest writings the verse, based on the ten-syllabled, five-beat iambic pentameter, is highly patterned. Rhetorical devices deriving from classical literature, such as alliteration and antithesis, extended similes and elaborate wordplay, abound. Often, as in *Love's Labour's Lost* and *A Midsummer Night's Dream*, he uses rhyming patterns associated with lyric poetry, each line self-contained in sense, the prose as well as the verse employing elaborate figures of speech. Writing at a time of linguistic ferment, Shakespeare frequently imports Latinisms into English, coining words such as abstemious, addiction, incarnadine and adjunct. He was also heavily influenced by the eloquent translations of the Bible in both the Bishops' and the Geneva versions. As his experience grows, his verse and prose become more supple, the patterning less apparent, more ready to accommo-date the rhythms of ordinary speech, more colloquial in diction, as in the speeches of the Nurse in *Romeo and Juliet*, the characterful prose of Falstaff and Hamlet's soliloquies. The effect is of increasing psychological realism, reaching its greatest heights in *Hamlet*, *Othello*, *King Lear*, *Macbeth* and *Antony and Cleopatra*. Gradually he discovered ways of adapting the regular beat of the pentameter to make it an infinitely flexible instrument for matching thought with feeling. Towards the end of his career, in plays such as *The Winter's Tale*, *Cymbeline* and *The Tempest*, he adopts a more highly mannered style, in keeping with the more overtly symbolical and emblem-atical mode in which he is writing.

So far as we know, Shakespeare lived in Stratford till after his marriage to Anne Hathaway, eight years his senior, in 1582. They had three children: a daughter, Susanna, born in 1583 within six months of their marriage, and twins, Hamnet and Judith, born in 1585. The next seven years of Shakespeare's life are virtually a blank. Theories that he may have been, for instance, a school-master, or a lawyer, or a soldier, or a sailor, lack evidence to support them. The first reference to him in print, in Robert Greene's pamphlet *Greene's Groatsworth of Wit* of 1592, parodies a line from *Henry VI, Part III*, implying that Shakespeare was already an established playwright. It seems likely that at some unknown point after the birth of his twins he joined a theatre company and gained experience as both actor and writer in the provinces and London. The London theatres closed because of plague in 1593 and 1594; and during these years, perhaps recog-nizing the need for an alternative career, he wrote and published the narrative poems *Venus and Adonis* and *The Rape of Lucrece*. These are the only works we can be certain that Shakespeare himself was responsible for putting into print. Each bears the author's dedication to Henry Wriothesley, Earl of Southampton (1573–1624), the second in warmer terms than the first. Southampton, younger than Shakespeare by ten years, is the only person to whom he personally dedicated works. The Earl may have been a close friend, perhaps even the beautiful and adored young man whom Shakespeare celebrates in his *Sonnets*.

The resumption of playing after the plague years saw the founding of the Lord Chamberlain's Men, a company to which Shakespeare was to belong for the rest of his career, as actor, shareholder and playwright. No other dramatist of the period had so stable a relationship with a single company. Shakespeare knew the actors for whom he was writing and the conditions in which they performed. The permanent company was made up of around twelve to fourteen players, but one actor often played more than one role in a play and additional actors were hired as needed. Led by the tragedian Richard Burbage (1568–1619) and, initially, the comic actor Will Kemp (d. 1603), they rapidly achieved a high reputation, and when King James I succeeded Queen Elizabeth I in 1603 they were renamed as the King's Men. All the women's parts were played by boys; there is no evidence that any female role was ever played by a male actor over the age of about eighteen. Shakespeare had enough confidence in his boys to write for them long and demanding roles such as Rosalind (who, like other heroines of the romantic comedies, is disguised as a boy for much of the action) in *As You Like It*, Lady Macbeth and Cleopatra. But there are far more fathers than mothers, sons than daughters, in his plays, few if any of which require more than the company's normal complement of three or four boys.

The company played primarily in London's public playhouses – there were almost none that we know of in the rest of the country – initially in the Theatre, built in Shoreditch in 1576, and from 1599 in the Globe, on Bankside. These were wooden, more or less circular structures, open to the air, with a thrust stage surmounted by a canopy and jutting into the area where spectators who paid one penny stood, and surrounded by galleries where it was possible to be seated on payment of an additional penny. Though properties such as cauldrons, stocks, artificial trees or beds could indicate locality, there was no representational scenery. Sound effects such as flourishes of trumpets, music both martial and amorous, and accompaniments to songs were provided by the company's musicians. Actors entered through doors in the back wall of the stage. Above it was a balconied area that could represent the walls of a town (as in *King John*), or a castle (as in *Richard II*), and indeed a balcony (as in *Romeo and Juliet*). In 1609 the company also acquired the use of the Blackfriars, a smaller, indoor theatre to which admission was more expensive, and which permitted the use of more spectacular stage effects such as the descent of Jupiter on an eagle in *Cymbeline* and of goddesses in *The Tempest*. And they would frequently perform before the court in royal residences and, on their regular tours into the provinces, in non-theatrical spaces such as inns, guild-halls and the great halls of country houses.

Early in his career Shakespeare may have worked in collaboration, perhaps with Thomas Nashe (1567–*c.* 1601) in *Henry VI, Part I* and with George Peele (1556–96) in *Titus Andronicus*. And towards the end he collaborated with George Wilkins (*fl.* 1604–8) in *Pericles*, and with his younger colleagues Thomas Middleton (1580–1627), in *Timon of Athens*, and John Fletcher (1579–1625), in *Henry*

VIII, *The Two Noble Kinsmen* and the lost play *Cardenio*. Shakespeare's output dwindled in his last years, and he died in 1616 in Stratford, where he owned a fine house, New Place, and much land. His only son had died at the age of eleven, in 1596, and his last descendant died in 1670. New Place was destroyed in the eighteenth century but the other Stratford houses associated with his life are maintained and displayed to the public by the Shakespeare Birthplace Trust.

One of the most remarkable features of Shakespeare's plays is their intellectual and emotional scope. They span a great range from the lightest of comedies, such as *The Two Gentlemen of Verona* and *The Comedy of Errors*, to the profoundest of tragedies, such as *King Lear* and *Macbeth*. He maintained an output of around two plays a year, ringing the changes between comic and serious. All his comedies have serious elements: Shylock, in *The Merchant of Venice*, almost reaches tragic dimensions, and *Measure for Measure* is profoundly serious in its examination of moral problems. Equally, none of his tragedies is without humour: Hamlet is as witty as any of his comic heroes, *Macbeth* has its Porter, and *King Lear* its Fool. His greatest comic character, Falstaff, inhabits the history plays and *Henry V* ends with a marriage, while *Henry VI, Part III*, *Richard II* and *Richard III* culminate in the tragic deaths of their protagonists.

Although in performance Shakespeare's characters can give the impression of a superabundant reality, he is not a naturalistic dramatist. None of his plays is explicitly set in his own time. The action of few of them (except for the English histories) is set even partly in England (exceptions are *The Merry Wives of Windsor* and the Induction to *The Taming of the Shrew*). Italy is his favoured location. Most of his principal story-lines derive from printed writings; but the structuring and translation of these narratives into dramatic terms is Shakespeare's own, and he invents much additional material. Most of the plays contain elements of myth and legend, and many derive from ancient or more recent history or from romantic tales of ancient times and faraway places. All reflect his reading, often in close detail. Holinshed's *Chronicles* (1577, revised 1587), a great compendium of English, Scottish and Irish history, provided material for his English history plays. The *Lives of the Noble Grecians and Romans* by the Greek writer Plutarch, finely translated into English from the French by Sir Thomas North in 1579, provided much of the narrative material, and also a mass of verbal detail, for his plays about Roman history. Some plays are closely based on shorter individual works: *As You Like It*, for instance, on the novel *Rosalynde* (1590) by his near-contemporary Thomas Lodge (1558–1625), *The Winter's Tale* on *Pandosto* (1588) by his old rival Robert Greene (1558–92) and *Othello* on a story by the Italian Giraldi Cinthio (1504–73). And the language of his plays is permeated by the Bible, the Book of Common Prayer and the proverbial sayings of his day.

Shakespeare was popular with his contemporaries, but his commitment to the theatre and to the plays in performance is demonstrated by the fact that only about half of his plays appeared in print in his lifetime, in slim paperback volumes known as quartos, so called because they were made from printers' sheets folded twice to form four leaves (eight pages). None of them shows any sign that he was involved in their publication. For him, performance was the primary means of publication. The most frequently reprinted of his works were the non-dramatic poems – the erotic *Venus and Adonis* and the more moralistic *The Rape of Lucrece*. The *Sonnets*, which appeared in 1609, under his name but possibly without his consent, were less successful, perhaps because the vogue for sonnet sequences, which peaked in the 1590s, had passed by then. They were not reprinted until 1640, and then only in garbled form along with poems by other writers. Happily, in 1623, seven years after he died, his colleagues John Heminges (1556–1630) and Henry Condell (d. 1627) published his collected plays, including eighteen that had not previously appeared in print, in the first Folio, whose name derives from the fact that the printers' sheets were folded only once to produce two leaves (four pages). Some of the quarto editions are badly printed, and the fact that some plays exist in two, or even three, early versions creates problems for editors. These are discussed in the Account of the Text in each volume of this series.

Shakespeare's plays continued in the repertoire until the Puritans closed the theatres in 1642. When performances resumed after the Restoration of the monarchy in 1660 many of the plays were not to the taste of the times, especially because their mingling of genres and failure to meet the requirements of poetic justice offended against the dictates of neoclassicism. Some, such as *The Tempest* (changed by John Dryden and William Davenant in 1667 to suit contemporary taste), *King Lear* (to which Nahum Tate gave a happy ending in 1681) and *Richard III* (heavily adapted by Colley Cibber in 1700 as a vehicle for his own talents), were extensively rewritten; others fell into neglect. Slowly they regained their place in the repertoire, and they continued to be reprinted, but it was not until the great actor David Garrick (1717–79) organized a spectacular jubilee in Stratford in 1769 that Shakespeare began to be regarded as a transcendental genius. Garrick's idolatry prefigured the enthusiasm of critics such as Samuel Taylor Coleridge (1772–1834) and William Hazlitt (1778–1830). Gradually Shakespeare's reputation spread abroad, to Germany, America, France and to other European countries.

During the nineteenth century, though the plays were generally still performed in heavily adapted or abbreviated versions, a large body of scholarship and criticism began to amass. Partly as a result of a general swing in education away from the teaching of Greek and Roman texts and towards literature written in English, Shakespeare became the object of intensive study in schools and universities. In the theatre, important turning points were the work in England of two theatre directors, William Poel (1852–1934) and his disciple Harley Granville-Barker (1877–1946), who showed that the application of knowledge, some of it newly acquired, of early staging conditions to performance of the plays could render the original texts viable in terms of the modern theatre. During the twentieth century appreciation of Shakespeare's work, encouraged by the availability of audio, film and video versions of the plays, spread around the world to such an extent that he can now be claimed as a global author.

The influence of Shakespeare's works permeates the English language. Phrases from his plays and poems – 'a tower of strength', 'green-eyed jealousy', 'a foregone conclusion' – are on the lips of people who may never have read him. They have inspired composers of songs, orchestral music and operas; painters and sculptors; poets, novelists and film-makers. Allusions to him appear in pop songs, in advertisements and in television shows. Some of his characters – Romeo and Juliet, Falstaff, Shylock and Hamlet – have acquired mythic status. He is valued for his humanity, his psychological insight, his wit and humour, his lyricism, his mastery of language, his ability to excite, surprise, move and, in the widest sense of the word, entertain audiences. He is the greatest of poets, but he is essentially a dramatic poet. Though his plays have much to offer to readers, they exist fully only in performance. In these volumes we offer individual introductions, notes on language and on specific points of the text, suggestions for further reading and information about how each work has been edited. In addition we include accounts of the ways in which successive generations of interpreters and audiences have responded to challenges and rewards offered by the plays. The Penguin Shakespeare series aspires to remove obstacles to understanding and to make pleasurable the reading of the work of the man who has done more than most to make us understand what it is to be human.

                                        Stanley Wells

The Chronology of Shakespeare's Works

A few of Shakespeare's writings can be fairly precisely dated. An allusion to the Earl of Essex in the chorus to Act V of *Henry V*, for instance, could only have been written in 1599. But for many of the plays we have only vague information, such as the date of publication, which may have occurred long after composition, the date of a performance, which may not have been the first, or a list in Francis Meres's book *Palladis Tamia*, published in 1598, which tells us only that the plays listed there must have been written by that year. The chronology of the early plays is particularly difficult to establish. Not everyone would agree that the first part of *Henry VI* was written after the third, for instance, or *Romeo and Juliet* before *A Midsummer Night's Dream*. The following table is based on the 'Canon and Chronology' section in *William Shakespeare: A Textual Companion*, by Stanley Wells and Gary Taylor, with John Jowett and William Montgomery (1987), where more detailed information and discussion may be found.

The Two Gentlemen of Verona	1590–91
The Taming of the Shrew	1590–91
Henry VI, Part II	1591
Henry VI, Part III	1591

Henry VI, Part I (perhaps with Thomas Nashe)	1592
Titus Andronicus (perhaps with George Peele)	1592
Richard III	1592–3
Venus and Adonis (poem)	1592–3
The Rape of Lucrece (poem)	1593–4
The Comedy of Errors	1594
Love's Labour's Lost	1594–5
Edward III (authorship uncertain, not included in this series)	not later than 1595 (printed in 1596)
Richard II	1595
Romeo and Juliet	1595
A Midsummer Night's Dream	1595
King John	1596
The Merchant of Venice	1596–7
Henry IV, Part I	1596–7
The Merry Wives of Windsor	1597–8
Henry IV, Part II	1597–8
Much Ado About Nothing	1598
Henry V	1598–9
Julius Caesar	1599
As You Like It	1599–1600
Hamlet	1600–1601
Twelfth Night	1600–1601
'The Phoenix and the Turtle' (poem)	by 1601
Troilus and Cressida	1602
The Sonnets (poems)	1593–1603 and later
Measure for Measure	1603
A Lover's Complaint (poem)	1603–4
Sir Thomas More (in part, not included in this series)	1603–4
Othello	1603–4
All's Well That Ends Well	1604–5
Timon of Athens (with Thomas Middleton)	1605
King Lear	1605–6

Introduction

ANTI-SEMITISM AND RACISM

In 1973 the Anglo-Jewish playwright Arnold Wesker reached a decision about *The Merchant of Venice*:

I ceased finally to be a 'forgiver' when . . ., watching Laurence Olivier's oi-yoi-yoi portrayal of Shylock in Jonathan Miller's production at the National Theatre, I was struck by the play's irredeemable anti-Semitism . . . Here was a play which, despite the poetic genius of its author – or who knows, perhaps because of it! – could emerge as nothing other than a confirmation of the Jew as bloodsucker. (*The Merchant*, ed. Glenda Leeming)

Wesker's solution to his anger with Shakespeare's play was to write a new version of the narrative, one in which Shylock is a good man and a close friend of Antonio, the merchant of Shakespeare's title. For Wesker, Shakespeare's Shylock, the Jew who pursues to the courtroom his right to exact a pound of Antonio's flesh as penalty for late repayment of a loan, was the epitome of a Western anti-Semitic portrayal of the Jew as evil villain concerned only with money. The result in *The Merchant* (first performed in 1976) is that, when Portia makes clear in the courtroom that he cannot cut his pound of flesh, Wesker's Shylock is hugely relieved.

Turning the plot of a Shakespeare play upside down is a recurrent practice of adapters, particularly when their own perspective – cultural, political or historical – makes what they see as Shakespeare's view or the view that is dominant at a particular moment completely unacceptable. But with *The Merchant of Venice* apparent rewriting of the plot began very early indeed. The title page of the first edition of the play, published in 1600, announces that the play includes 'the extreme cruelty of Shylock the Jew towards the said merchant in cutting a just pound of his flesh'. A purchaser of this version of the play-text might have expected Shylock to be successful in his appalling revenge.

Probably the compositor who set the title page or whoever wrote out the title-page copy from which the printer worked made the mistake simply because he had not read the play, but the very first reference to the play to survive, the record of the payment by the publisher to establish his right to print the play, suggests that there was some disagreement about what the play's title was: the 'Merchant of Venice, or Otherwise Called the Jew of Venice'. Rather than being a subtitle, this other name for the play suggests that, from the beginning, it was Shylock who had the greatest impact on playgoers. In the climactic trial scene the rich heiress Portia, disguised as a lawyer, asks, 'Which is the merchant here? And which the Jew?' (IV.1.171), and, when the Duke orders them to stand forth and she asks, 'Is your name Shylock?', some productions have her ask the question of the wrong man, necessitating a correction from Shylock: 'Shylock is my name' (with the emphasis on 'my'). But her possible confusion is shared more widely: generations of students of this play have needed to be told that Shylock is not the merchant of the title.

Be it the consequences of the Holocaust or the crises in the Middle East, we are today particularly aware of anti-Semitism. The way Shylock is presented onstage, a topic I explore in The Play in Performance, is a matter of anxiety and concern. What one playgoer finds acceptable another may find deeply offensive. In the desperate struggle to keep Antonio alive, Venice's own lawyers cannot find the loophole that saves him. It is Portia, the outsider from the fictional Belmont, who has to remind the Duke in the courtroom that Venice has harsh penalties especially reserved for any of its 'alien' population who attempts to kill a Venetian citizen. Shakespeare's Venice is a city which legislates its discrimination against its outsiders, the non-Venetians who live, work and trade there. But its laws might need to be set against Portia's treatment of her Moroccan suitor, the first of her onstage wooers to undertake the test her dead father has imposed in his will: that whoever wishes to marry Portia must choose the right one of three caskets (gold, silver or lead). Her final comment after he chooses the wrong casket, the golden one, 'Let all of his complexion choose me so' (II.7.79), cannot but be heard as an echo of his first line, 'Mislike me not for my complexion' (II.1.1), the two lines bracketing his presence in the play with his invitation to her to look at him more than skin-deep now turned into her apparently deep racism. Unpalatable though it may be, Portia offers the same white Christian perspective and solution to the problem of the play's two characters who represent racial and religious otherness onstage.

MONEY AND COMMERCE IN VENICE

But, however we respond to the racial and religious politics of the play, the context within which they are presented is dominated by money. As the play's title implies, more than any other Shakespeare play *The Merchant of Venice* is a drama particularly concerned with money and commerce. While the world of Belmont, that Shakespeare invents to set against the reality of early modern Venice, is an expanse that draws the world's suitors to it to gain control of the fabulous wealth Portia has inherited, in Venice, the trading capital of Europe, the wealth of Antonio the merchant is the product of risky international trade. Eligible bachelors come from Morocco and Spain, from Naples and France, from England, Scotland and Germany – as well as from Venice – to woo her. Antonio's ships travel out from Venice across the world: to Tripoli and the Indies, to Mexico and England, and elsewhere. He is as careful in his venture capitalism as he can be, spreading the risk, holding resources in reserve:

> My ventures are not in one bottom trusted,
> Nor to one place; nor is my whole estate
> Upon the fortune of this present year. (I.1.42–4)

Portia is the magnet, the force that creates this energy that magnetically draws men to her. Antonio is the power that sends his heavily laden trading ships, his 'argosies', out across the world, in the hope and expectation that they will return to the centre, Venice, and give it and him yet more power.

Shylock's wealth, presumably like that of Tubal and Chus, 'his countrymen' (III.2.285), is the product of moneylending. Money begets money. When Shylock retells to Antonio and Bassanio the biblical narrative of Jacob and the sheep in Act I, scene 3 Antonio wonders why: 'Was this inserted to make interest good? | Or is your gold and silver ewes and rams?' (91–2). There are two puns on 'ewes', both on 'Jews' and on 'use', for Jews put money out to use and become wealthy through this interest; as Shylock replies, 'I cannot tell, I make it breed as fast' (93). In Shylock's dealings money becomes procreative and, restricted from most other ways of making money (for Jews could not trade freely), this Jew's trading with money stands as a kind of perversion of sexuality, as manipulative as Jacob, whose trick with the ewes increased his wealth.

But it is not only the Jews whose business seems a mixture of money and sex. Shakespeare's Venice is a distinctly odd place as a city of trade. Antonio is the only Christian merchant we see onstage. All the other men are gentlemen, not merchants. Modern productions often set the first scene of the play in some kind of bar or restaurant or tavern, and when they do it is always Antonio who is seen to be paying for everyone else. Gentlemen in Venice have no money. They may have inherited wealth but they have spent it and need to find a way to replace it, usually by marrying money, be it Portia in Belmont or Jessica in Venice. Women are a commodity to be traded in the play, since they bring with them their caskets, whether the three caskets between which Portia's suitors must choose or the one full of Shylock's gold and jewels that his daughter, Jessica, carries from her father's house as she elopes.

What is also strange about this Venice is its overwhelming maleness. There are no Christian women referred to at any point. None of the men appears to be married. The only family seems to be Shylock's, with his dead wife, Leah, and his living daughter, Jessica; and the latter's marriage to a gentile will make him yearn for her death: 'Would she were hearsed at my foot' (III.1.81–2). Jessica's escape from her father's oppressive household, her rejection of her family, race and religion, is achieved through her outward transformation of her gender, joining the male world of Christian Venice, for she meets Lorenzo and his friends disguised as a boy. In exchanging her father's house for her future husband's, Jessica takes part in the play's systems of exchange and trade, the substituting of one thing for another, the commodification and metamorphoses that are central to the merchant's business. In any case, as Launcelot Gobbo, the play's comic servant (first Shylock's, later Bassanio's man), argues, even religious conversion has economic consequences, for by converting Jessica to Christianity and thereby increasing the number of Christians, Lorenzo has also 'raise[d] the price of pork' (III.5.32). In the dialogue that follows (33–6) Lorenzo reminds Launcelot that he has made the 'Moor' pregnant by raising 'the Negro's belly' (Shakespeare does not distinguish between the two races). The play never gives this black woman a name, never makes her visible, never brings her onto the stage, but the conversation conjures up the only other woman who seems to live in Venice, another racial stranger, a woman whom Launcelot can dismiss as only a prostitute. Faith, sex and pork are only aspects of trade or, at least, are implicated in it.

CURRENCY AND EXCHANGE RATES

Whatever else may be being traded and exchanged in *The Merchant of Venice*, the only currency in which value is expressed in monetary terms is ducats. Shakespeare uses the term 'ducat' and its plural fifty-nine times in ten plays; thirty-three of these occurrences are in *The Merchant of Venice*. It is one of the units of currency in Illyria (*Twelfth Night*), Italy (for example in *Cymbeline*), Denmark (*Hamlet*) and Ephesus (*The Comedy of Errors*). It is also referred to in *The Two Gentlemen of Verona*, *Romeo and Juliet*, *Much Ado About Nothing*, *Measure for Measure* and *The Taming of the Shrew*.

Ducats were Italian coins but they also circulated in England so that Shakespeare's audience would have had as clear a concept of their value as a modern audience in England would have of dollars or euros. Some ducats showed Christ on the reverse face, the possible source of Shylock's reported reference to his 'Christian ducats' (II.8.16). There were silver ducats but the Venetian coins of *The Merchant of Venice* are almost certainly gold, whose value varied between about eight and eleven shillings (in modern coinage between 40p and 55p). Then as now the exchange rate depended on when and where you changed your currency. As Antonio Salutati, the author of a merchant's manual, commented in 1416: 'He who deals in exchanges and he who deals in merchandise is always anxious and beset by worries. I will instead give you a recipe for lasagna and macaroni.' (quoted in Frederic C. Lane and Reinhold C. Mueller, *Money and Banking in Medieval and Renaissance Venice*, vol. 2, *The Venetian Money Market* (1997)). But as a rough guide a rate of two ducats to the pound seems to be right. Insofar as one can tell from the references, Shakespeare seems to have maintained a consistent sense of its value, roughly equivalent to the exchange rate.

What the sum might mean in modern terms is much more difficult to calculate – calculations based on notions of inflation are always difficult. Three thousand ducats, the value of the loan Shylock makes to Antonio in *The Merchant of Venice*, was the annual income of Sir Andrew Aguecheek and represented a sum worthy of a gentleman (*Twelfth Night*, I.3.20), as indeed it should, for the audiences would have heard the figure as equal to approximately £1,500 a year, a sign of very considerable wealth at a time when the Stratford schoolmaster was paid £20 a year with room and board. If we multiply early values by about 250, it will give a reasonable idea of the minimum the sums are now worth. Sir Andrew Aguecheek's capital earned him at least £375,000 a year.

In the economic commerce of *The Merchant of Venice*, with its contracts and penalty clauses, its bills for dinner or for a diamond, its generous offers from betrothed to future husband and its crucial, central fascination with a loan, the value of money is of very great importance indeed. For as the references to ducats proliferate in the play they begin to suggest a coherent economic and fiscal system by which each sum of money can be weighed and valued, a system of difference and connection in which the sums take on a life of their own, as if money were a strangely creative force in the play.

PENALTIES AND USURY

When the news reaches Belmont that Antonio could not pay his bond when it came due and that Shylock is intending to exact the penalty for late payment of a pound of flesh Salerio makes clear that Shylock will no longer accept the repayment of the sum: 'it should appear that if he had | The present money to discharge the Jew, | He would not take it' (III.2.272–4). As Shylock himself makes clear in the trial scene, having the pound of Antonio's flesh is worth the loss of the sum of the bond: 'The pound of flesh which I demand of him | Is dearly bought' (IV.1.99–100), the last phrase significantly echoing Portia's valuation of Bassanio's love for her in relation to the monetary gift she offers to make to him to settle Antonio's debts: 'Since you are dear bought, I will love you dear' (III.2.313). This pound of human meat costs Shylock 3,000 ducats or 6,600 ducats per kilo.

Indeed it would not matter to Shylock if he were offered more. As Jessica tells the gathering at Belmont:

> . . . I have heard him swear
> To Tubal and to Chus, his countrymen,
> That he would rather have Antonio's flesh
> Than twenty times the value of the sum
> That he did owe him . . . (III.2.284–8)

Shylock will not accept 60,000 ducats – or at least that is the largest sum he can imagine refusing in order to kill Antonio. Worth in modern terms not less than £7.5 million, this vast amount represents the limits of Shylock's imaginings, a fantastical excess of over-repayment. Repaying the principal twenty times for a bond after three months represents an astonishing 8,000 per cent base annual rate of interest. There is no sign, of course, that Shylock is a loan shark; there is no indication that he charges high rates of interest. Antonio's practice of lending out money with no interest charges has an effect on the interest rates the Jewish moneylenders can charge: 'He lends out money gratis and brings down | The rate of usance here with us in Venice' (I.3.41–2). This clearly rankles with Shylock. He makes a similar comment later, when warning Antonio's friends 'Let him look to his bond', 'He was wont to lend money for a Christian courtesy' (III.1.44–5). But at this point too, for the only time in the play, the explicit accusation of usury surfaces: 'He was wont to call me usurer' (43). 'Usance', a word Shylock uses three times in Act I, scene 3, like Antonio's statement to the court that Shylock should 'let me have | The other half [of his wealth] in use' (IV.1.379–80), is a word that connects with usury but without its long history of pejorative overtones of excessive and illegal rates. Shylock is clearly especially furious that Antonio frequently calls him usurer, for it was a serious charge.

USURY AND THE LAW

The bond between Shylock and Antonio is not in fact a matter of usury. The pound of flesh is a penalty payment, not a matter of interest. The bond would have stood at no risk under English law on usury, in particular the Statute of 1571, which defined English legal principles at the time Shakespeare wrote *The Merchant of Venice*. Though the Bible banned all interest charges as usury, English law recognized a difference between allowable charges and illegal higher rates: any bond that charged interest at more than 10 per cent was automatically nullified under this act, which, however, did not stop some individuals from continuing to charge extortionate rates. Shakespeare might have remembered his family's first-hand experience of the impact of the statute: in 1570, when Shakespeare was six, his father, John Shakespeare, was twice accused of breaking the law on usury by charging interest of £20 on a loan of £80 and another of £100, both to a business associate, and was once fined £2 as a result. But Shylock's bond would have been acceptable under English laws on interest rates.

But would a contract with its penalty of the pound of flesh have been legal under other aspects of English law? In the courtroom scene Shakespeare may well be dramatizing the tension between two systems of English law: common law, which depended on statute and precedent, and equity, the province of the Court of Chancery, where decisions were based on less precise concepts of natural justice and conscience. Portia's plea for 'mercy' might have sounded as an appeal to equity. Perhaps the argument over whether a contract should be honoured and how its terms should be executed might also have seemed to spectators at the Globe like the kind of matter, carried to extreme, that was the province of yet another branch of the contemporary English legal system, the Staple Court in London. This was set up specifically to deal with trade disputes with foreign merchants, yet was able to become a criminal court when occasion required, just as the Venetian court becomes one when the dispute over the contract turns into a case of attempted murder.

VENICE AND BELMONT

The courtroom drama has an edge of immediacy, not only of dramatic suspense but also of a relation to a world experienced outside the theatre, that rarely forms a significant part of Portia's Belmont, a fantasy space aligned by Bassanio at the play's opening with the mythical quest of Jason for the golden fleece:

> . . . her sunny locks
> Hang on her temples like a golden fleece,
> Which makes her seat of Belmont Colchos' strond,
> And many Jasons come in quest of her. (I.1.169–72)

However heavily the weight of Portia's father's will hangs over her choice of husband and however much the audience comprehends her entrapment by a patriarchal system, Belmont nonetheless seems nearer to the setting for a romantic fairy tale than Venice ever does.

Much of the play's movement between its twin locations can depend on how far playgoers would have viewed the events of the plot as dissociated from an English reality, simply part of a fantasy or foreignness that then defines what kind of play this is. Renaissance Venice was seen, from the perspective of Renaissance London, as a place unlike home, a city of danger as well as wealth, a warning of the kind of city London might become. Venice's influence was declining, just as London's economic power was increasing. Would London's control of the world's trade also one day start to wane? However Londoners compared the two cities, at the same time they could see Shakespeare's Venice as a depiction of a real city, an urban environment that could always be seen as like the reality of life in London in some ways. Belmont could be seen as nothing but fantasy. In part, the Belmont side of the action, the winning of Portia through the right choice between the three caskets, comes from an old tradition, the narrative of the choice of three – something that Shakespeare would return to in *King Lear* (as Lear chooses between his three daughters), a choice which Freud aligned with *The Merchant of Venice* in his essay on 'The Theme of the Three Caskets' and analysed as the choice of death. Versions of the casket-story date back to the ninth century; Shakespeare probably knew it from a medieval collection, the *Gesta Romanorum*, some of which had been published in translation in 1577 and (revised) in 1595. Shakespeare seems to have used this last edition, turning to a new book for the old story.

JEWS

The tale of the bond of flesh may be equally old and Shakespeare would have known, in the original or a close translation, a version by the Florentine author Ser Giovanni, which appears in a collection of tales called *Il Pecorone*, written in the late fourteenth century but first published in Milan in 1558. Like those of almost all his plays, Shakespeare's plot for *The Merchant of Venice* is not original. If the legal concerns of the courtroom link this ancient plot more immediately to London, it is not only the Venetian setting that keeps the narrative at a certain distance. So, too, does the story's concern with a villainous Jew, for Jews were even more alien to Shakespeare's London than to the play's Venice. Officially expelled from England in 1290 by Edward I, there were nonetheless some Jews living in early modern England, ostensibly as converts though some were probably Marranos, who were outwardly Christian but continued to practise their religion secretly. Demonized by popular belief and onstage often the source of dramatic evil, there were few positive images of Jews to set against the culture of antagonism towards these supposedly damned souls. Though Robert Wilson's play *The Three Ladies of London* (1584) had shown a good and generous Jew, Gerontus, opposed by a comic villain, an Italian merchant who would rather convert to Islam than pay his debts to the Jew – a plot which might find its echo in the enforced conversion of Shylock at the end of the court scene – there was no shortage of Jewish villains to offset this apparently lone example of Jewish goodness. Christopher Marlowe's popular play *The Jew of Malta* was written around 1589, revived in 1594 and played frequently in

1596 by the Lord Admiral's Men, the leading rivals to the Lord Chamberlain's Men, the company in which Shakespeare was a sharer. Indeed, Shakespeare's play may be his company's response to the continued success of the opposition with Marlowe's. Barabas, the Jew of Marlowe's title, may be a dramatic means of exposing the corruption of the Christians of Malta but that hardly diminishes the evil of his murderous behaviour. There were vicious Jews in other plays too, and in narratives like Thomas Nashe's *The Unfortunate Traveller* (1594).

Queen Elizabeth's physician, Roderigo Lopez, had been a converted Portuguese Jew but he was executed in 1594 when found guilty of complicity in a Jesuit plot to murder the queen. Lopez was probably not attacked as a Jew at his trial nor mocked as a Jew on his way to the gallows, as once supposed, and his original Jewish faith may not even have been widely known. There is ample evidence that in English courts Jews were treated fairly before the law, including the Portuguese Jews who in 1596, close to the date of the first performances of *The Merchant of Venice*, were sued by the widow of an English merchant for whom they had acted as agents. Those Jews who lived in London experienced a reasonable degree of toleration from the Christian state and its citizens, provided they outwardly conformed enough, with genuine freedom to carry on trades and professions and to practise their religion at home. There was nothing in London to match the Venetian Ghetto, that area of Venice where Jews were forced to live and into which they were locked at night. Venice had given the word ghetto to the world; London seemed by comparison a place of reasonable tolerance. The English were also curious about Jewish practices, reported by foreign travellers like Thomas Coryat, whose account of the Jews in Venice and of a Jewish circumcision rite was published in 1611, some years after Shakespeare's play had been staged and published. But the association of Jews with religious damnation, with occult and probably evil practices, with financial greed and with a vicious antagonism towards all things Christian still pervaded popular culture. As so often, local tolerance and popular mythology were deeply at variance.

But it is not enough simply to identify Shylock as a Jew and therefore as standing for everything that is non-Christian. The name Shylock itself may hint at other resonances. The name might possibly be derived from the Hebrew word *shellach*, meaning a cormorant, a standard term of abuse for usurers, or from Shiloch or Shiloh or Shelach or Shelah or any of the other Hebrew names scholars have suggested as its source. But it was also an English name, meaning white-haired, like Whitlock and Whitehead, and it is possible that there were Shylocks living in Shakespeare's London just as there are still. Shylock as a name for a moneylender might just as easily have been suggestive of an Englishman as a Venetian Jew. While Jews were linked to usury, the Christian justification of charging interest was part of the interconnection between Protestantism and capitalism, for John Calvin himself had argued for the significance of credit. The legal acceptance of interest, turning the sin of usury into something legally justifiable, provided it was not at too high a rate, was necessary for the smooth functioning of the early modern English state.

In any case, Shylock does not stand for all Jews, even within the play. In performance Tubal may explicitly reject Shylock's actions, showing his revenge to be explicitly unacceptable to the only other male Jew in the play. Jessica rejects her father too. In the court Shylock enters alone, not surrounded by fellow Jews. The loss of his daughter as well as of his money may have driven him beyond the bounds of social acceptance by his own community. His antagonism to Antonio in Act I, scene 3 is certainly inflamed by Antonio's anti-Semitism ('He hates our sacred nation', 45) as well as by the effect of Antonio's actions on his profit margin, but it is not here explicitly focused on murder.

It is not clear at this stage that the contract is designed to achieve Antonio's death at all and the terms of the contract mysteriously metamorphose in the course of the play. At first the pound of flesh is 'to be cut off and taken | In what part of your body pleaseth me' (I.3.147–8). Shakespeare and some of his audience may well have known the version of the narrative in Alexander Silvayn's *The Orator*, a translation of which was published in 1596, in which the Jew argues that he might cut off 'his privy members, supposing that the same would altogether weigh a just pound'. Castration, as a mockingly extreme version of circumcision, may have been in this Jew's mind and perhaps in Shylock's. But by the time the action reaches the courtroom the terms of the contract's stipulation of the pound are now explicit: Portia can only confirm that the pound of flesh is stipulated as being 'Nearest the merchant's heart' (IV.1.230).

Shylock, receiving the news that Antonio has lost his ventures, had earlier ordered Tubal to arrange for his enemy's arrest, for 'I will have the heart of him if he forfeit' (III.1.116–17), but the phrase sounds like a generalized threat not a specific intent to carve out Antonio's heart. Shylock's search for profit ('for were he out of Venice | I can make what merchandise I will', 117–18) makes it sound less likely that murder is Shylock's meaning. The audience may wonder whether even a man like Shylock can seriously intend to kill to increase his freedom to trade.

By the time of the court scene, however, the word 'heart' takes on a terrible literalness. 'Heart', with all its cognates, will be spoken twenty-seven times in the play and has been heard twenty times already but often in conventional phrases in which we hardly hear its meaning: saying 'with all my heart' (III.2.195 or III.4.35) has no strong sense of the physical body. Now its implications become unnervingly clear. For St Paul, rethinking phrases in the Old Testament book of Deuteronomy, the Christian version of circumcision was not outward but inward, not of the foreskin but of the heart, an invisible circumcision of the spirit, an alteration that would be known only to the individual and to God, who alone would test its truth. Shylock turns the Pauline doctrine inside out. He will cut around the heart and the flesh is intended, as he told Salerio, to 'feed my revenge' (III.1.49), for what Shylock sees the Jews as learning from the Christians is the practice of revenge.

Shylock's speech in Act III, scene 1 in defence of his action has often been read as a humane statement for tolerance. Certainly he begins from his identification of Antonio's motives as straightforward anti-Semitism: 'and what's his reason? I am a Jew' (52–3). But from an itemized listing of the common humanity that Jews and Christians share Shylock moves to accept the Christian lesson of the shared human motive of revenge:

> If a Jew wrong a Christian, what is his humility? Revenge. If a Christian wrong a Jew, what should his sufferance be by Christian example? Why, revenge! The villainy you teach me I will execute, and it shall go hard but I will better the instruction. (62–6)

Having hands and eyes in common is one thing, but there is no requirement that the (im)moral lessons of one religious group should be learned by the members of another. Being human does not require the right to revenge. Indeed, Christianity, with its doctrine of turning the other cheek, is explicitly based on a rejection of what it saw as the Old Testament's commitment to an eye for an eye, the equity of revenge. If these Christians have been behaving in an unchristian way, that does not justify Shylock.

LOVE AND WEALTH IN BELMONT

As so often in *The Merchant of Venice*, Shakespeare sets up a pattern that asks us to compare what happens in Venice with what happens in Belmont, to compare the moral values of the two locations, to wonder whether women and men behave differently. The taking of the pound of flesh in the Shylock part of the plot is set against the giving of one's heart in the love of Portia and Bassanio, two people who, like Antonio, are caught by the letter of a legal document – the will of Portia's father, which imposed the casket test. Shortly before Jessica tells the assembled company at Belmont that her father will not take 60,000 ducats ('twenty times the value of the sum | That he did owe him', III.2.287–8), Shakespeare had allowed the numbers 60 and 1,000 to be heard in the scene in Portia's extravagantly modest wish to be far fairer and richer, to be many times herself for Bassanio:

> . . . yet for you
> I would be trebled twenty times myself,
> A thousand times more fair, ten thousand times
> More rich, that only to stand high in your account,

> I might in virtues, beauties, livings, friends,
> Exceed account . . . (152–7)

But though Portia's multiplication tables include wealth, it seems an abstracted conceptualization of number, not something translatable into the practice of Venetian or Belmontese economics. This sense of number is part of the fantasy of Belmont, the place where the choice of the right casket, the box in which the image of Portia lies, will be accompanied with a song wondering about where fancy is placed: 'Tell me where is fancy bred, | Or in the heart, or in the head?' (III.2.63–4). With Jessica's statement it is newly grounded in the reality of Shylock's commitment to his bond. This vast sum is now the value Shylock places on his revenge.

Jessica makes her statement as forthrightly as she can but Portia seems to have some difficulty taking in the information. Perhaps she is simply not listening to the account; perhaps she only now understands the implication of Jessica's twice mentioning Antonio by name (286, 290). Certainly Jessica's statement is not responded to directly, for the line which follows it, spoken by Portia, is addressed not to Jessica but to Bassanio: 'Is it your dear friend that is thus in trouble?' (291). The hiatus here between statements might be significant. There are many ways to play it: she may, for instance, be deliberately ignoring the Jewish woman's words, for the Portia who dislikes the Prince of Morocco's complexion might well also be anti-Semitic and nobody in the group has so much as mentioned Jessica, silent till this speech, since Gratiano identified her at her entrance as Lorenzo's 'infidel' (218). But, however it is played, the gap, the refusal of the normal mechanism of dialogue – statement and response – needs noting and playing. In that gap the notion of this

sum of money is translated into a definition of social
inter-relationship, the understanding of how the two
women, Jewess and heiress, interact.

When Portia does turn to the question of the sum the
riches of Belmont become apparent. We have known from
the first mention of her – by Bassanio to Antonio in the
first scene – that Portia has been 'richly left' (I.1.161),
that she has inherited a considerable fortune from her
father. That may have been manifest in modern productions in the opulence of the set for the Belmont scenes.
At this point in the play it becomes explicitly stated in
terms of monetary value. Finding that the debt is three
thousand ducats, Portia replies:

> What, no more?
> Pay him six thousand, and deface the bond.
> Double six thousand and then treble that,
> Before a friend of this description
> Shall lose a hair through Bassanio's fault. (III.2.298–302)

After the wedding is solemnized, even before it is consum-
mated, Portia suggests that Bassanio should rush off to
Venice: 'You shall have gold | To pay the petty debt twenty
times over' (306–7). It all depends what one means by
'petty'. Portia finally offers Bassanio precisely the sum that
Jessica has already said Shylock will turn down. It had
been difficult for Antonio to raise as much as 3,000 ducats
anywhere in Venice, including, we assume, from Christian
sources – hence his willingness to turn to the hated Shylock.
Even Shylock says – though some productions have
implied that it may not be true – that he cannot, in his
present financial circumstances, lay his hands immediately
on the money ('I cannot instantly raise up the gross | Of
full three thousand ducats', I.3.52–3). But Portia has no

hesitation in offering 60,000. 'Richly left' indeed, and we can see both how much she generously loves Bassanio and how much her father's wealth amounted to.

HUMANITY AND WEALTH IN VENICE

Along the way, though, if the audience's mental arithmetic keeps up with her lavishness, she offers a sum of 36,000 ('Double six thousand and then treble that', III.2.300), and the same figure is mentioned in the trial scene. Bassanio offers Shylock 6,000 ducats, the first figure that Portia mooted as sufficient to 'deface the bond', which sum he has presumably borrowed from Portia anticipating, foolishly, that it would be enough to assuage Shylock's demand for vengeance. If we have developed from the first scene a notion of Bassanio as prodigal and wastrel, a spendthrift who has run through his fortune and is now dependent on the generosity of Antonio to go a-wiving in the style he thinks appropriate, then it is offset by a certain caution here or an assumption that he understands money and human nature well enough to know that 6,000 ducats would be sufficient to satisfy Shylock's greed. Bassanio's notion of extravagance is, in this circumstance, quite circumspect, taking just enough of his newly acquired wealth to do what he thinks is possible but unwilling now to go the whole way and use such a large figure as Portia offered, whatever it may be as a proportion of her wealth, to deal with the Jew.

But Shylock rejects the offer:

If every ducat in six thousand ducats
Were in six parts, and every part a ducat,
I would not draw them. I would have my bond. (IV.1.85–7)

The imaginary sums of ducats conjured up by the dialogue and the idea of what can be done with them now seem to have become strangely creative and fertile, transferring from Belmont to Venice without any apparent means, magically transporting themselves from Portia's thought to Shylock's. Money as a concept is fluid and transient at exactly the point in the play at which, intransigent and intractable as he is at his most extreme, Shylock refuses to allow any transfer of sums at all. As the idea of what constitutes a lavish sum moves from Venice to Belmont and back to Venice, so the money itself is bound up in Shylock's hatred and the operation of justice. It all depends now on Shylock's willingness to accept any sum, on his evaluation of the reasons to be merciful, given that there is no legal compulsion on him to accept the money. Indeed the law is as immovable as Shylock: Bassanio's suggestion that the law for once can be flexible and malleable in dealing with the diabolic Shylock ('Wrest once the law to your authority, | To do a great right, do a little wrong, | And curb this cruel devil of his will', IV.1.212–14) shocks Portia in her disguise as the lawyer Balthasar: 'It must not be' (215).

Shylock's refusal makes it impossible to break the original agreement which had locked the sum in an interest-free contract and defined the non-financial penalty for defaulting. Significantly, Shylock, identified as usurer by Antonio, did not charge Antonio interest on the loan. As a gesture of feigned friendship, he has offered the sum interest free, behaving as Antonio does towards fellow Christians:

I would be friends with you and have your love,
Forget the shames that you have stained me with,

> Supply your present wants, and take no doit
> Of usance for my moneys, and you'll not hear me.
> This is kind I offer. (I.3.135–9)

Bassanio's reply picks up, perhaps suspiciously, on that crucial last word: 'This were kindness' (140). 'Kind' and 'kindness' are a common Shakespearian pun. Shylock means both that he will be benevolent and generous and that he will be of Antonio's kind, like him in 'lend[ing] out money gratis' (41), that the Jew is capable of and willing to behave like a Christian. Far from belonging to a necessarily other group, a subset of humanity – or indeed what Antonio seems to conceive of as a set of subhumanity – the group of Jews who are unable ever to be like Christians, Shylock offers something else, a form of integration: his effective assimilation into the manners and ethics of the dominant Venetian culture through an acceptance of their business practices in this one offer at least. It is a notion of 'kind' keyed into this discussion through Shylock's elaborate description of the way Jacob made his fortune with the ewes, a process in which sex between rams and ewes becomes defined as natural, what we might call now 'species-specific' and which Shakespeare calls 'the deed of kind' (82).

LOANS AND SECURITY

But there is a further problem, hinted at in Shylock's statement about where he will find the additional part of the three thousand ducats that he does not have available: 'Tubal, a wealthy Hebrew of my tribe, | Will furnish me' (I.3.54–5). One of the crucial biblical passages on

usury is in Deuteronomy (23: 19–20), here quoted from
the Geneva Bible of 1587, one of the translations Shakespeare is likely to have known:

Thou shalt not give to usury to thy brother, as usury of money,
usury of meat, usury of any thing that is put to usury.
Unto a stranger thou mayest lend upon usury, but thou shalt
not lend upon usury unto thy brother, that the Lord thy God
may bless thee in all that thou settest thine hand to in the land
whither thou goest to possess it.

The marginal gloss to the phrase about lending to a
stranger reads 'This was permitted for a time for the
hardness of [the Jews'] heart', a reminder of the depth
of antagonism to usury and the conventional linkage of
Jews and usury, even at a point where the Bible explicitly permits it. When Shylock borrows money from
Tubal, a member of his tribe, a 'brother' in the sense
that the biblical phrase implies, Tubal would be unable
to charge Shylock interest, even though the eventual
destination of the money is Antonio – or properly
Bassanio. Of course there will be nothing remotely like
a legal agreement for that loan between the two
Christians: it is a bargain between a merchant and a
Christian gentleman, a gentleman's agreement, a loan
with no security other than Bassanio's sense of his obligation to Antonio. That class difference between Antonio
and the other Venetian Christians to which I referred
earlier exemplifies in this loan the way in which
gentlemen, in Venice or in England, lived upon credit
and merchants found it difficult to get their bills paid.
Whatever the emotional link between the two men,
Bassanio owes Antonio 'the most in money and in love'
(I.1.131) – and some actors who play Bassanio add the

second phrase hastily to cover up the awkward reduction of their relationship to debts. But that bond, whether of intense friendship or sexual desire, whether shared or only one-way, whether homosocial or homoerotic, is hardly likely to prove as strong even as Shylock's bond.

In any case, the best security that Bassanio can offer here is no better than the accuracy of his aim with arrows:

> In my schooldays, when I had lost one shaft,
> I shot his fellow of the self-same flight
> The self-same way, with more advisèd watch,
> To find the other forth; and by adventuring both
> I oft found both. (140–44)

This image of Bassanio's is the only real economic justification or security he can offer Antonio to justify Antonio's pouring yet more money into (or, more accurately, through) Bassanio's hands. The argument is doubly unconvincing: firstly, it is simply an account of a frequent but not consistent solution ('I *oft* found both'); secondly, it is a false account of what happens in archery, for, archers tell me, the schoolboy who mistakes his aim will be unable accurately to repeat the mistake on any but the rarest of occasions – and many of Shakespeare's playgoers were trained archers who would immediately see the false reasoning.

Bassanio admits he is doubly Antonio's debtor, 'in money and in love'. Both debts will need repaying, love as well as money or, perhaps, that love from Antonio to Bassanio, the love of an older man for a younger, which Bassanio has used or abused to create a debt of money. But Antonio is far from being Bassanio's only creditor and some of his other debts have – he hints – a more substantial obligation:

> . . . my chief care
> Is to come fairly off from the great debts
> Wherein my time, something too prodigal,
> Hath left me gaged. (I.1.127–30)

The word 'gaged' indicates that Bassanio is bound, as
Antonio will be. What happens to a Venetian gentleman
like Bassanio, unlike the fate of a merchant such as
Antonio, when he fails to meet the due date of his other
debts is far from clear in the play. Gentlemen, especially
gentlemen with no other form of income than their inherited wealth and no intention of working for a living even
by the trade of mercantile speculation, live on credit.
Antonio's letter to Bassanio indicates that when a
merchant falls on hard times all credit is called in: '*my
creditors grow cruel*' (III.2.316) writes Antonio, and we
have to assume that Shylock is the only Jew amongst
them. Bassanio has plainly continued to find ways of
living well, even though he has run out of cash.

Characteristically of the play, however, the language
of economics affects Bassanio's description to Antonio
at the play's beginning of his style of living; he has:

> . . . disabled my estate
> By something showing a more swelling port
> Than my faint means would grant continuance.
> Nor do I now make moan to be abridged
> From such a noble rate . . . (I.1.123–7)

Usually 'rate' is glossed as 'style' but the word also
suggests a rate of expenditure in the commercial world
of Venice. Shylock speaks of Antonio bringing down
'The rate of usance here with us in Venice' (I.3.42); the

Prince of Morocco wonders whether he is 'rated by thy estimation' (II.7.26); Bassanio, trying to explain his poverty to Portia, speaks of 'Rating myself at nothing' (III.2.257). A word intrinsically bound up with finance is here appropriated by and appropriate to the nature of gentlemanly and gentile existence, living at 'a noble rate'.

But the word spirals outwards, as so often with Shakespeare's language, for Antonio's attitude towards Shylock is also a matter of 'rate': not long after he has spoken in aside about 'the rate of usance' Shylock uses both nouns again, separated a little more widely in a sentence:

> Signor Antonio, many a time and oft
> In the Rialto you have *rated* me
> About my moneys and my *usances*. (I.3.103–5; my italics)

Now 'rate', changed from noun to verb, carries the notion of opprobrium: Antonio berates Shylock for his rate of usance. One man's interest rates deserve another man's berating; Shylock's rate turns him into a loan shark or, to extend the bad pun that Shylock had already stretched to its limits, 'land thieves, I mean pi*rates*' (23; my italics).

Antonio's argosies are at risk from pirates and storms, rocks and waves. Risky though such ventures could be, Antonio has been both extravagant and cautious. It may be that much of his wealth is bound up in these ventures, that he has no liquidity, no monetary assets and indeed no assets sufficiently assured to enable others to use them as security for a loan. But he has chosen to spread the risk. As Shylock reminds Bassanio in the scene where the loan is set up, 'He hath an argosy bound to Tripolis, another to the Indies; I understand, moreover, upon the

Rialto, he hath a third at Mexico, a fourth for England, and other ventures he hath squandered abroad' (I.3.17–21). Squandering is significant: Shylock suggests that the ventures are too risky, the kind of venture that would be almost bound to lead to inevitable loss and catastrophe. Antonio, at this point, appears a little like Bassanio – another figure who has squandered his wealth incautiously. But such enterprises could also produce phenomenal profits, a return on investment of many thousand per cent, far beyond anything that usury or the simple charging of non-usurious interest could expect. It may have been something of a lottery but there were plenty of examples in England of merchants who had grown fantastically rich on the profits of a single such voyage. Venture capitalism in a context of mercantilist culture was a risky but often remarkably successful route to wealth.

Viewed in this way, Antonio's sending out his argosies to trade is remarkably similar to the reason why Bassanio needs to borrow the 3,000 ducats in the first place. The journey to Belmont is a sea-voyage, a speculative enterprise. Unlike Antonio, who spreads the risk by having a whole series of different ships out at sea, a fleet of ventures, Bassanio will sink all his – or rather Antonio's – money in one last-ditch effort to extricate himself from debt. The journey to Belmont becomes, in Bassanio's first description of it, an epic quest, a voyage premised on the similarity of the appearance of Portia's hair to the object of the journey of Jason and the argonauts. Portia becomes nothing more than a mythic object to be won; her hair becomes the fleece and nothing more religious than a part of her head becomes the temple where it was hanging: 'her sunny locks | Hang on her temples like a golden fleece' (I.1.169–70). When Bassanio chooses aright in the lottery (another speculative venture like those of Antonio's argosies), Gratiano comments, 'We are the Jasons, we have won the Fleece' (III.2.241), and the image returns. Perhaps it is a language that Bassanio would only use in private to Antonio, a kind of demeaning assessment of the meaning of his enterprise that he would never voice aloud to Portia – but no such notion of tact inhibits Gratiano.

EXTRAVAGANCE AND THRIFT

But what exactly does Bassanio need the money for? There is a striking difference between the epic quest that Bassanio seems to be undertaking in venturing from Venice to Belmont and the kind of journey from Padua to Venice that Portia describes when instructing her servant Balthasar to visit the lawyer Bellario:

> . . . look what notes and garments he doth give thee
> Bring them, I pray thee, with imagined speed
> Unto the traject, to the common ferry
> Which trades to Venice. (III.4.51–4)

There seems to be a regular public transport system of *traghetti*, the Italian word for 'ferries' which Shakespeare anglicizes as 'traject'. Where Bassanio needs to be decked out at the right 'noble rate' for this great questing journey, dressed in the style to which he has been accustomed and in which he hopes marriage to Portia will maintain him, Portia suggests a rather different way of navigating these ventures: one simply checks the timetable and catches the next ferry.

Portia's own journey to Venice, initially in the comfort

of her coach 'which stays for us | At the park gate' (III.4.82–3), may be in disguise but this is not like the dangerous journey in disguise that Rosalind makes to Arden in *As You Like It* or the desperate disguise of the shipwrecked Viola in *Twelfth Night*. There may be risks of embarrassing discovery or equally embarrassing failure in the courtroom but nothing more threatening than that. Portia's long description to Nerissa of herself playing a man makes it sound like a carnival disguising, a performance that she can carry off effectively (60–78). While Rosalind became Ganymede, the name of Jove's cup-bearer, Portia simply usurps her servant's name and becomes Balthasar (so that one may wonder what name Balthasar himself uses when he arrives in Venice).

Bassanio, whose stylish voyage will cost the modern equivalent of hundreds of thousands of pounds to set up, does not need such extravagant expenditure to enter the lottery of the caskets. The commitment he needs to make is not the stake money for a wager but the willingness to accept the conditions of the casket choice: never to divulge the secret and to remain single thereafter. He chooses to spend money, not to impress Portia but to 'hold a rival place' (I.1.174) with the other Jasons, to look their equal. Once Bassanio has secured the loan money we see him using it to ensure his servants will represent his status properly at Belmont, instructing a servant to 'put the liveries to making' (II.2.107), with his new servant Gobbo having an especially striking outfit, 'a livery More | guarded than his fellows'' (143–4). Bassanio has other uses for the money for which Antonio has so dangerously bound himself: he will spend some of it on a 'supper' (105–6), a farewell party before the voyage at which he will 'feast tonight | My best-esteemed acquaintance' (159–60).

Such extravagance among his fellows in Venice, like the proper appearance among his rivals in Belmont, is for Bassanio the right way of spending Antonio's loan. As far as he is concerned, this male rivalry is what matters and the expenditure in the quest looks to him like 'thrift': 'I have a mind presages me such thrift | That I should questionless be fortunate' (I.1.175–6).

We will hear the word 'thrift' again later in the play and the cluster of meaning that surrounds it is another part of the play's valuation of the language of money. Three of its occurrences will come from Shylock. In that long aside about Antonio's hatred, he complains that Antonio rails 'On me, my bargains, and my well-won thrift' (I.3.47). He ends his description of Jacob's tricking Laban with the statement 'thrift is blessing if men steal it not' (87). And talking with Jessica, he uses the word in another rather glib moral cliché: 'Fast bind, fast find, | A proverb never stale in thrifty mind' (II.5.52–3). Making a profit is, for Shylock, a matter of thrift.

Being careful with one's resources is, of course, a good lesson for anyone wanting to be thrifty. One meaning of thrift is being economical with one's assets: as Hamlet tells Horatio about the rapid sequence of his father's funeral and his mother's remarriage: 'Thrift, thrift, Horatio. The funeral baked meats | Did coldly furnish forth the marriage tables' (I.2.180–81). But that is not quite what Shylock means. 'Thrift' here in *The Merchant of Venice* is allowed to connect to its cognate verb, 'to thrive'. Where 'thrift' might suggest being frugal, 'thrive' might suggest to Bassanio being extravagant; certainly for Shylock it suggests being hugely successful. For Shylock the two may come together: as Shylock says of Jacob's stratagem, 'This was a way to thrive, and he was blest' (I.3.86). Like Bassanio's use of 'thrift', thrifty thriving is a way to be 'fortunate' and Jacob's trick is a profitable enterprise.

If you make the right – that is, thrifty – choice you should thrive but gold is not necessarily the way to thrift and thriving. A later appearance of the word is at the end of Morocco's speech of choice. He chooses the golden casket: 'Here do I choose, and thrive I as I may!' (II.7.60). The meagre choice of lead, the thriftiest substance used in the manufacture of the caskets, proves to be the thriving one. Bassanio's journey will be thrifty in the sense that it will be profitable but the way to achieve it is, for Bassanio, to ensure that he continues to appear at the same 'noble rate' that had got him into financial trouble before.

There is here an ambiguity about how one uses one's resources that is central to the conflict of care and extravagance in the play. For Bassanio to be truly thrifty he must *'give and hazard all he hath'*, as the lead casket proclaims (II.7.16), venturing everything to gain the golden fleece. It suggests the problem in the play's final use of thrift. In the moonlit scene at Belmont, as Lorenzo and Jessica wait for Portia's return, they exchange comparisons with failed loves in classical stories: Troilus and Cressida, Pyramus and Thisbe, Dido and Aeneas, Medea and Jason. Then Lorenzo teases – or taunts – Jessica with their own story:

> In such a night
> Did Jessica steal from the wealthy Jew,
> And with an unthrift love did run from Venice
> As far as Belmont. (V.1.14–17)

Lorenzo's language is disconcertingly ambiguous: does Jessica 'steal' away from Shylock or does she steal money from him? Is the 'unthrift love' Jessica's careless, absolute love for Lorenzo, or is the 'love' Lorenzo himself, a spend-thrift like Bassanio who perhaps needs Jessica's wealth as much as, or even more than, he needs Jessica?

The financing of Bassanio's venture also affects another word, another part of the commercial language that suggests a system of value. As Shylock, in conver-sation with Bassanio, considers whether Antonio is a reasonable risk, he comments to Bassanio, 'Antonio is a good man' (1.3.12). Bassanio bridles at the suggestion that he might be anything else: 'Have you heard any impu-tation to the contrary?' (13–14). Shylock has to spell out to this unbusinesslike man what he means by 'good': 'Ho no, no, no, no! My meaning in saying he is a good man is to have you understand me that he is sufficient' (15–17). Being 'sufficient' is to have sufficient sums available, to be solvent not bankrupt like Bassanio, to be affluent, well-to-do. It is not only a question of Antonio's status but also of whether he is a decent business risk. Morality, at least in the way that Bassanio hears 'good', is bound here to the language of business. Whether Antonio is virtuous or not, kind, generous, good-hearted or any other meaning of the word in conventional moral terms is irrelevant to good business practices. Shylock is concerned only with whether Antonio is good for the money's repayment.

BETTING ON SEX

The play offers other ways of making money than mercantile speculation or charging high rates of interest. One way is betting; Portia will 'hold thee [Nerissa] any wager, | . . . I'll prove the prettier fellow of the two'

(III.4.62, 64). Just before the threat posed by Shylock bursts into the restrained world of Belmont Gratiano suggests that fertility can be a way of making money fertile, making it as creative as the sexual activity he and Nerissa will enjoy as man and wife: 'We'll play with them, the first boy for a thousand ducats' (III.2.213–14). Nerissa is hesitant about how the wager will be set up: 'What, and stake down?' (215). Her meaning, that the money would have to be laid on the table for the wager to be valid, is taken in a different way by her future husband: 'No, we shall ne'er win at that sport, and stake down' (216–17). Typically Gratiano turns her financial argument into a sexual pun, for he plays on the sense of 'stake down' meaning 'with a limp penis'. If he cannot get an erection, the son – worth a thousand ducats – will never be conceived. Making money in this context is an expression of masculinity.

In Gratiano's language such wordplay on sexual meanings is frequent. In all kinds of ways there is nothing elsewhere in Shakespeare's drama quite like the end of this play, but the fact that it gives its final lines to Gratiano may be more than a little unnerving. No other Shakespearian comedy ends with such a directly dirty joke: 'Well, while I live I'll fear no other thing | So sore as keeping safe Nerissa's ring' (V.1.306–7). By 'ring' he means both the one on her finger and her vulva – the line alludes to an old joke, which assumes that the right way, indeed the only way, for a husband to keep his wife faithful is not to keep her ring on one's finger but to keep a finger inserted in her vagina.

There is nothing romantic in this final image. Gratiano's pun is horribly reductive. The language of love has become the language of male fear of uncontrollable female sexual activity. Instead of allowing an

unmediated focus on the rings that have moved from
finger to finger throughout the later part of the play,
Shakespeare requires that we become startlingly aware
of Nerissa's genitals. Modern productions usually baulk
at the implications of this, preferring to leave the pun
undefined and the attention of the audience looking at
the ring now back on Gratiano's finger, but the pun is
actively there, a threat to the kinds of emotions of love
prevalent in the Portia–Bassanio relationship. In its sala-
cious punning it demeans the romantic world of Belmont,
a reminder of the laddish, loutish, all-male culture of
Venice to which Gratiano – and Bassanio – belong.

PORTIA'S RING

The circulation and exchanges of Portia's and Nerissa's
rings connects with another ring in the play, another
circle of prodigality and rejection of thrift, as well as
another precise sum of ducats. As Shylock laments to
Tubal the loss of his money and his daughter, Tubal
passes on two pieces of news about Jessica's activities.
'Your daughter spent in Genoa, as I heard, one night
fourscore ducats.' Shylock is tormented by the news:
'Thou stick'st a dagger in me. I shall never see my gold
again. Fourscore ducats at a sitting, fourscore ducats!'
(III.1.98–102). But worse is to follow: one of Antonio's
creditors showed Tubal 'a ring that he had of your
daughter for a monkey' (108–9).

SHYLOCK Out upon her! Thou torturest me, Tubal. It was my
    turquoise; I had it of Leah when I was a bachelor. I would
    not have given it for a wilderness of monkeys. (110–13)

The two pieces of news are strikingly different. The first
is a simple mark of extravagance and of the impossi-
bility of Shylock's ever recovering all his gold. He has
lost money and jewels; one of the jewels, a diamond,
'cost me two thousand ducats in Frankfurt' (III.1.77).
Using the exchange rate I have suggested we can value
the diamond at a quarter of a million pounds. Jessica's
dinner at Genoa would have cost at least £10,000. Such
estim-ates of value are significant for our understanding
of the meaning of the sums quoted: if the sums Portia
offers Bassanio seem to us massive and extravagant they
are heard in relation to other sums, the sums that belong
to Venice as it were, that are large but not fantastical. It
does not follow that Portia's huge wealth therefore
becomes part of a fairy tale, even though it would put
her on any list of the world's richest people. Bassanio
carries a part of that wealth into the courtroom and the
audience sees the 6,000 ducats he offers (though paper
money will look rather different from a pile of gold
coins).

Similarly, Jessica's restaurant bill of £10,000 must
affect how we evaluate Shylock's reaction. If a ducat
were worth considerably less, then Shylock's horror at
the expenditure of 'fourscore . . . at a sitting' might point
to his stinginess. He could be accused of being not only
a usurer but also a miser. But with these sums in mind
the shock is unsurprising, even reasonable: children,
whether they have stolen the money from their parents
or not, are not supposed to spend at 'such a noble rate'
(I.1.127). This is expenditure in Bassanio's league. How
Shylock reacts might also be defined by what we have
seen of Shylock's own use of his money, something that
will vary in performance. Some Shylocks dress richly,
wealthy men who parade their wealth; others can be the

epitome of miserliness. But even for a Shylock willing to spend money on himself, the fourscore ducats that Jessica has spent might well seem extravagant, far beyond even his comfortable lifestyle.

We talk of objects having 'sentimental value' as well as monetary value, and if 'sentimental' is a word we are wary of, then in this context it may have a precise and deeply painful sense. Robbery reminds us of that which cannot be expressed in value, of the meanings we attach to objects in ways that insurance companies do not comprehend, those signs of our parents and grand-parents that, whatever the objects' insured value, are beyond price for us.

Rings have a special potency in this economic system of value and its denial, as signs of the linking of people together in marriage bonds. The giving of a ring was, in Shakespeare's time, significant enough an event for courts to accept it as firm proof of betrothal even in the absence of other evidence. In *Cymbeline*, as in *The Merchant of Venice*, the plot runs on the value placed on a ring. Posthumus moves from prizing or pricing his wife Imogen and the symbol of her, his ring, at 'More than the world enjoys' (I.4.75) into accepting that the ring – and hence Imogen – can have precise value. He makes a wager with the villain Jachimo on Imogen's chastity, in which he lays the ring against Jachimo's ten thousand ducats (I.4.128–9).

When Portia, after the trial scene, tries to wheedle her ring out of Bassanio, he recognizes a distinction between its monetary worth and its meaning as a token of love: 'There's more depends on this than on the value' (IV.1.431). He may be recalling, as the audience perhaps ought, that earlier, when Portia had transferred it to him, she had defined the full range of its potent meanings:

This house, these servants, and this same myself
Are yours, my lord's. I give them with this ring,
Which when you part from, lose, or give away,
Let it presage the ruin of your love
And be my vantage to exclaim on you. (III.2.170–74)

The ring signifies a transfer of wealth, of status, of love
and, not least important, of Portia herself, a woman
trapped, through the exchange processes of patriarchy,
in the transition between father and husband, rescued,
by Bassanio's choice of casket, from the limbo of being
unattached to any man except the 'will of a dead father'
(I.2.24). Hence, confronted by Portia's, or rather
'Balthasar's', pressing request, Bassanio offers instead:
'The dearest ring in Venice will I give you, | And find
it out by proclamation' (IV.1.432–3). Money, here, is no
object; he will spend anything but not pass over the ring.
In the end he agrees, giving in to Antonio's request, which
deliberately sets in opposition the values Antonio places
on the two sides of Bassanio's life:

My Lord Bassanio, let him have the ring.
Let his deservings, and my love withal,
Be valued 'gainst your wife's commandèment. (446–8)

Antonio carefully balances the deservings and love on
the one hand and the orders of a wife on the other, a
deliberately unequal equation.

At the climax of the trial scene, just as he was about
to face Shylock's knife, Antonio had pointedly linked his
farewell to his intrusion in Bassanio's relationship to
Portia:

> Commend me to your honourable wife,
> Tell her the process of Antonio's end,
> Say how I loved you . . . (IV.1.270–72)

The rhythm of the start of the last line is tricky: is it in iambics, an instruction to describe the manner of the love ('Say *how* I *loved* you'), or is it in trochees, an emphasis that he should speak of Antonio's love for Bassanio rather than hers ('*Say* how *I* loved *you*')? Antonio compares two loves, his own and Portia's for the same man.

In response, Bassanio outlines a vision of value that goes beyond the precision of economics, something outside the exchange systems by which value is defined:

> Antonio, I am married to a wife
> Which is as dear to me as life itself,
> But life itself, my wife, and all the world
> Are not with me esteemed above thy life.
> I would lose all, ay sacrifice them all
> Here to this devil, to deliver you. (279–84)

Portia's list of the wealth embodied in the ring is precise and meaningful in a commercial structure, 'This house, these servants, and this same myself'. Bassanio's is not; it stretches to things he cannot give, like 'all the world'. No wonder that Portia's response is wry: 'Your wife would give you little thanks for that | If she were by to hear you make the offer' (285–6).

The value Bassanio or Antonio might place on their relationship – however we read the degree of active homoerotic desire on either part between them – is one that could threaten Bassanio's marriage to Portia. In the eccentric and intriguing production by the American director Peter Sellars for the Goodman Theatre in Chicago in 1994, Portia did not at the end of the play hand over to Antonio a sealed letter announcing the safe return of three argosies, a moment of blatant artifice in the plot, which Shakespeare underlines with her comment, 'You shall not know by what strange accident | I chancèd on this letter' (V.i.278–9). Sellars had her calmly write out a large cheque and give it to Antonio, a clear indication that he should get out of her husband's life and stay out. There was no room in this marriage for Antonio's love.

JESSICA'S RING

Let me return, finally, to Jessica's theft of Shylock's ring. Shylock's distress at the loss of the turquoise has nothing to do with its monetary value. He does not price it. Instead he gives it a history, places it in relation to his life. Patrick Stewart, analysing his own performance as Shylock (in *Players of Shakespeare 1*, ed. Philip Brockbank), described it as a 'simple gift, possibly a betrothal ring, from a woman to her lover'. I would remove the hesitation over 'possibly'. The ring is heard as the gift that defined the betrothal of Leah to Shylock 'when I was a bachelor' (III.i.111–12). It marked Shylock's future wife's love for him and hence, in the value he attaches to it, his love for his wife. For Stewart much was contained in that word 'bachelor':

That word shatters our image of this man Shylock and we see the man that once was, a bachelor . . . Shakespeare doesn't need to write a pre-history of Shylock. Those two lines say it all.

It is striking how this lost youth points to the over-whelming sense of loss that surrounds Shylock. Leah, like many Shakespearian wives and mothers, is invisible, unseen and largely unknown but it is difficult to hear in Shylock's lines anything other than love and pain, the two emotions captured together in the 'wilderness', the arid world inhabited only by chattering monkeys, those Elizabethan symbols of lust. Jessica's pet seems a pecu-liarly cruel substitute for the ring and the substitution itself, the choice of selling that ring, is a mark of her cruelty. For it is surely unlikely that Jessica did not know the meaning of the ring, the token of betrothal, the link between her parents. Her theft can be seen as another of the play's acts of vengeance, a response to the hell she finds her father's house to be ('Our house is hell', II.3.2).

In escaping from that oppression, Jessica exchanges her father for a husband, Lorenzo. Rather than being passed passively from one male hand to another, she chooses to control her own act of social mobility by marriage. Perhaps she deserves her Lorenzo, the man who, after Jessica has praised Portia to the skies, can only respond by praising himself, 'Even such a husband | Hast thou of me as she is for a wife' (III.5.78–9), a strikingly tasteless piece of Venetian male arrogance. In the circu-lation of women in the play, Jessica makes a very specific intervention, claiming the right to make her own choice, one that is not available to Portia or at least one which Portia chooses not to accept as being within her control.

Jessica controls the meaning and value of her acts, but, like the effect of her conversion on the price of bacon, the implications start to spin out beyond her control. When the play shifts from Venice to Belmont for the last time, and the Jews vanish from the play, so only the ambivalence which Jessica represents is left; it is not clear whether she is Jew or Christian, left in a religious limbo of damnation, a token whose value is increasingly uncertain and whose position in the play is increasingly one of silence. By the end it is Portia who is controlling the activity, as the play's final ringmaster – until, that is, even she has to hand control back to the male view of female behaviour, a context within which rings no longer signify a value of ducats or a value beyond ducats but simply a value of sexual possession and male fear.

The Merchant of Venice gives the few women in its cast unusual power to act. In performance Portia often seems increasingly independent, finally freed from her father's will and certainly not subject to her husband's. In the fairy tale of Belmont, Shakespeare seems to be suggesting, such freedom may be possible. In the harsh reality of Venice women, when present at all, seem unable to do more than make ill-advised matches: Lorenzo and Jessica, Launcelot and his 'Moor'. Jessica's power there is restricted to stealing money and stealing away. If the end of the play allows some of the harshness of the economic world of Venice to recede into the distance when viewed from the very different perspective of Belmont, it does little to alleviate a rather gloomy view of the way men behave towards women and towards each other. The money problems of many of the characters, with the glaring exception of Shylock, have been solved: Bassanio, Lorenzo and Antonio all have wealth again. But beyond the play's end the problems of the relationships remain opaque and not particularly encouraging. Has Jessica made a poor bargain in choosing Lorenzo? What place will Antonio have in Bassanio's and Portia's marriage? Has Bassanio really reformed? Shakespeare leaves the members of the audience to make up their own minds: some may be confident about the characters' futures, others rather less so. By comparison with the problems of such relationships in Belmont, Venice's problems with money and with race seem positively straight-forward.

Peter Holland

The Play in Performance

The Merchant of Venice has been performed for over four hundred years and in virtually every part of the world. Its performance history, on stage, television, radio, audio-recording and film, is rich testimony to the ways in which actors, directors and designers have explored the choices it offers them, each making decisions based on the cultural and historical context of the production as well as on the interpretation of the text, the filling-in of the gaps and spaces that a printed Elizabethan play leaves. How might a line be spoken? How might an entrance be made? What kind of costume does a character wear? How are the actors placed across the stage's space? How do the players leave the stage? These questions have needed to be answered every single time the play is performed in the theatre, from the Globe in 1596 or 1597 to the present. They are problems that cannot be ignored. Every moment in performance is a product of decisions taken, whether by accident or design. An account of how some of those choices might affect our understanding of *The Merchant of Venice* allows us to explore the play both in the study and onstage, how the play's many possibilities have been and might be realized.

Since our memories and imaginings of a play in modern theatre tend to begin with sights, I want instead

to begin with two sounds, one in Belmont and one in
Venice. As Bassanio moves to make his choice from the
three caskets Portia orders 'Let music sound' (III.2.43),
and follows it with a long analysis of the significance of
music. The play is full both of music and of discussion
of its meaning and effects. There are flourishes for
entrance frequently throughout the play and at this point
Portia calls for music which turns out to be a song.
Lorenzo's description of the music as he and Jessica wait
for Portia (V.1.55–7 and 70–88) is so potent that Vaughan
Williams set part of it, most exquisitely, as his *Serenade
to Music*, and the dawn hymn that Lorenzo calls for also
resonates in the audience's ears. A production may make
its choice of music that the text does not call for speak
eloquently: Jonathan Miller ended his 1970 production
with Jessica alone onstage hearing the sound of Kaddish,
the Jewish prayer for the dead; Trevor Nunn ended his
in 1999 with Jessica, similarly alone, hearing the Hebrew
song in praise of the virtuous woman that her father had
sung in Act II, scene 5. The play's sound-score is bound
to be a highly significant part of the experience of the
play in performance.

But the song that the audience hears while Bassanio
chooses – or more usually, in performance, while he paces
around the caskets before beginning his long speech of
choice – is itself a problem. Its first rhymes – 'bred',
'head', 'nourishèd' – all encourage a link to 'lead', the
casket which Bassanio ought to choose. A setting which
hits the last word emphatically may make us aware of
the song as a hint. Its description of the funeral 'knell'
conjures up a lead coffin. Its message is a warning against
trusting the eyes, the source of 'fancy', and hence an
encouragement to look beyond the surfaces. If it is indeed
intended to tell Bassanio what choice to make, it is not

immediately successful and he still spends over thirty lines weighing up the decision. If Portia is cheating on her father's will, she would be, as she has told Bassanio, breaking her own oath ('I could teach you | How to choose right, but then I am forsworn', III.2.10–11). Directors must also decide whether to follow what was presumably the original choice of having a solo singer or whether to share it among a kind of onstage chorus, perhaps including Portia herself.

More significantly, this third scene of choosing among the caskets may mark the first time that Portia knows which one is the right one, putting new pressure on her to hint. While some Portias always know the right answer, others have been tense when Morocco chooses gold, having no idea whether he might be correct. An ignorant Portia may be encouraged when Arragon considers choosing gold but also finally relieved, after discovering what is in the silver casket, to know the answer to her father's riddle. She may be learning the solution as the audience does, and that can increase the dramatic tension in the earlier scenes. There has been no song for the other choices but, whether a hint is given or not, the agony of choice must still be endured – now only by Portia perhaps, since the audience knows both that lead is the right choice and, because it is that kind of play, that Bassanio will choose correctly.

The second sound to consider is the sound of Shylock's voice. A Shylock who sounds – as well as looks – different from the Venetian Christians may signal his alien status. It can reach extremes: Antony Sher (Royal Shakespeare Company, 1987) greeted Bassanio and Antonio in Act I, scene 3 while reclining on a low couch, turbaned and in flowing robes that marked him out as a Levantine Jew, his accent so thick as to be, at

times, difficult to understand. Ian McDiarmid, for the
RSC three years earlier, used an equally strong accent
but this time as if his natural language was Yiddish,
though a Venetian Jew's would not have been. When a
production alludes to a specific non-Renaissance period
the effect of the choice of voice may be even more
striking: Laurence Olivier (National Theatre, 1970) wore
false teeth and affected a clipped pronunciation that, by
dropping the final 'g' in, for example, 'speaking' or
'meaning', sounded like an attempt to ingratiate himself
with or assimilate to the upper-class voices of the
Christians. David Calder (RSC, 1993), in a production
set immediately contemporary, as if in the modern Stock
Exchange, complete with computers and mobile phones,
looked and sounded like the other Venetians but, asking
Antonio whether he should say 'Fair sir, you spat on me
on Wednesday last' (I.3.123), he dropped into a caricature of a Jewish accent as if to say, 'Is that how I ought
to sound?'

However Shylock sounds, his costume will probably
be a sign to the audience of how he fits or, more often,
does not belong comfortably alongside those who invite
him to dinner. We have little idea what the first Shylock
looked like: though there are many contemporary illus-
trations of Venetian Jews, there is no way of knowing
whether the Lord Chamberlain's Men costumed their
Shylock in that style. Olivier in his frock coat – the
production was set in the late nineteenth century – was
indistinguishable from the Christians until he removed
his top hat to reveal his skullcap. Calder, another assim-
ilated figure, was by the trial scene foregrounding his
new-found religious identity by wearing a skullcap.
Calder plainly wished to be accepted to exactly the same
extent that Antony Sher refused to be. The two Shylocks

directed by John Barton for the RSC, Patrick Stewart in 1978 and David Suchet in 1981, belonged to the same period but were at opposite extremes in the ways their costumes showed their attitudes to their wealth: Suchet in a stylish heavy overcoat was every inch the Rothschild millionaire tycoon, puffing on a big Havana cigar, wealthy and proud to show off his wealth; Stewart wore, in his own words, '[a] shabby black frock coat, torn at the hem and stained, a waistcoat dusted with cigarette ash, baggy black trousers, short in the leg, exposing down-at-heel old boots, and a collarless shirt yellowing with age', and smoked 'mean little hand-rolled cigarettes, whose butt-ends were safely stored away for future use'. As rich as Suchet's international banker, Stewart's Shylock was, above all, a miser, hoarding wealth for its own sake – and immediately far less sympathetic.

At the heart of the problem of playing Shylock is the degree of audience sympathy. In George Granville's adaptation of 1700 Shylock may be the title figure but he is a comic one. When Charles Macklin in 1741 created his ground-breaking interpretation of the character that would be the only Shylock seen in London for very nearly half a century he made Shylock a titanic villain, a man whose fierce malevolence was at times terrifying. Edmund Kean in 1814 was 'a decrepid old man, bent with age and ugly with mental deformity, grinning with deadly malice, with the venom of his heart congealed in the expression of his countenance', according to William Hazlitt (quoted by Charles Edelman, in his edition of the play), but there was something new too: the German writer Heinrich Heine, watching Kean, heard a woman in the audience announce loudly, 'The poor man is wronged', something no one would have said of Macklin's Shylock.

   Played by Henry Irving in 1879, the Jew was made to
look every inch the stranger in his Moroccan robes – for
it was the sight of a Moroccan Jew that made Irving
decide to play the role. But Irving's Jew was, in his own
analysis:

not a mere individual . . . [but] a type of the great, grand race
. . . a man famous on the Rialto; probably a foremost man in
his synagogue – proud of his descent – conscious of his moral
superiority to the Christians who scoffed at him, and fanatic
enough, as a religionist, to believe that his vengeance had in
it the element of godlike justice. (Quoted by James C. Bulman,
in his edition of the play)

This Shylock's torment was most marked in a famous
added piece of stage business – for such sequences typically place a performance – when, returning to his house
after dinner, he found it open and, realizing Jessica had
gone, he registered the most complete despair, which his
Portia, Ellen Terry, praised in her *Memoirs* (1932): 'For
absolute pathos, achieved by absolute simplicity of means,
I never saw anything in the theatre to compare with [it].'
This combination of pathos and pride throws Shylock's
tormentors into strong relief. For such a figure to be
forcibly converted to Christianity was a hideous piece of
mockery.

   Shylock's final exit is a moment that many actors have
used to underline their reading of the figure: Irving crum-
pled at the door as a broken old man; Olivier exited with
dignity but then the sound of his anguished howl came
from offstage, chilling the listeners onstage and in the
theatre; Stewart flipped off his skullcap with a compliant
laugh, grovellingly abject. When Philip Voss (RSC,
1997), who had slipped and fallen on the ducats Bassanio

had strewn across the floor, finally, awkwardly and painfully stumbled to his feet Gratiano maliciously grabbed the skullcap from his head; Shylock screamed, covered his head with his hands and was pushed offstage by Gratiano and Bassanio. Stewart resisted sympathy to the last; Voss never relinquished his demand that we sympathize. They played the same character but elicited diametrically opposite reactions from audiences, both towards them and, consequentially, towards their tormentors. Of course, the production's attitude may be profoundly affected by its context: the treatment of Shylock resonates differently in Nazi Germany or in post-Holocaust Israel. Directors can also ask audiences to reconsider what the Jew represents: Peter Sellars (Goodman Theatre, Chicago, 1994) cast African-American actors as the Jews, forthrightly demanding that we compare the treatment of one religious group with that of another ethnicity still oppressed in contemporary America.

Many of the characters can pose similar problems of response. Morocco may be a stereotyped and comic caricature or a serious man, overwhelmed by his realization of the arrogance that led to his mistake. Bassanio may stay a charming cad or mature to become worthy of Portia's love. Antonio may be a dignified man of substance or someone profoundly awkward in the company he keeps; he may be openly gay, and sad at the prospect of losing his lover, or, a concept far from the sensibilities of early modern England, he may be uncomfortable in his sexuality, and embarrassed by the emotional power his (possibly unreciprocated) desire for Bassanio exerts over his actions. Lorenzo may be endearing or arrogant, Gratiano funny or irritating. The other Venetian Christians, known in the theatre as the

'Salads' (a comic version of their names), may be gay
(as in Bill Alexander's 1987 production), they may be
racist and anti-Semitic or they may be neutral accompaniments to the main action.

Some productions put all their energies into Venice,
certainly the easier half of the play to stage, and forget
that the drama's shaping depends on a finely articulated
balance between the two worlds, an equilibrium that set
designers may aid in their representation of the two spaces
or make similarly unbalanced. For many years before
Irving's production star actors, playing Shylock, expected
the play to end after the trial scene with Act V cut
completely. How characters exist in the atmosphere of
Act V, particularly Jessica and Antonio, may be the means
for the play in performance to show whether such
outsiders, the previously Jewish woman and (in modern
terms) the homosexual man, can be newly incorporated
into the world of Belmont and Christian marriages or
whether they stay strangers. Where some Antonios may
exit at the end arm in arm with Bassanio and Portia,
others are left alone onstage, triumphant in their regained
wealth or despairing at their exclusion by the married
couple wrapped up in their love.

At the climax of the trial scene as Antonio prepares
for death and Shylock for revenge – and Antonios may
be reluctant or eager for death and Shylocks equally reluctant or eager to kill – Portia's three words, 'Tarry a little'
(IV.1.302), stop the action in its tracks and reverse the
entire movement of the scene. Portia's is by far the longest
role in the play and she is the controller of much of the
plot in the latter half. What makes her say at this point
'Tarry a little'? Often the actor has had to shout the
words over the sounds of Christian prayer (and even,
when Sher was accompanied by many Jews in the scene,

over the sound of Jewish liturgy). She may, like Peggy Ashcroft (Stratford, 1953), have to throw herself between Antonio and Shylock advancing with knife ready. Has she always known the solution, perhaps from Bellario, choosing only at the last moment to reveal it, the more to give Shylock the chance to change his mind and, perhaps, the more to make Antonio, her rival for Bassanio, suffer? Or has she been desperately scanning the bond or a law book, finally finding the unexpected answer?

The play, in the form we have it, cannot provide a clear answer, nor would we wish it to. *The Merchant of Venice* refuses to make such decisions for us. Instead, it leaves us the deep pleasure of weighing up different possibilities and their consequences: a Portia who always knew the escape clause is a very different individual from one who stumbles on it at the last second. A performance may show us ways of playing never before considered or confirm our previous assumptions. In its nearly inexhaustible range of choices from first to last, *The Merchant of Venice* renews our fascination with its dramatic meanings.

                                        Peter Holland

Further Reading

There are a number of fine modern facsimiles of the Quarto (Q1) of 1600, the first published text of the play, and of the first Folio (F1) of 1623, which derives from it. The most convenient facsimile version of Q1 is probably in *Shakespeare's Plays in Quarto*, edited by Michael J. B. Allen and Kenneth Muir (1981), and of F1 Charlton Hinman's carefully prepared edition, revised by Peter Blayney (1996). The section on the play in Stanley Wells and Gary Taylor's *William Shakespeare: A Textual Companion* (1987) is the best place to begin detailed study of the play's (limited) textual problems.

The Merchant of Venice has been lucky in its recent editors of scholarly editions: John Russell Brown's edition for the second series of the Arden Shakespeare (1955) is still useful but largely superseded by M. M. Mahood's New Cambridge Shakespeare edition (1987; updated 2003) and Jay L. Halio's Oxford Shakespeare edition (1993), both of which have long, comprehensive and splendid introductions. Editions with special concerns include Charles Edelman's excellent one for the Shakespeare in Production series (2002), by far the best place to study the stage history of the play, with a lengthy introduction and extensive commentary drawn from theatre history; M. Lindsay Kaplan's '*The Merchant of*

Venice': Texts and Contexts (2002), which reprints lengthy passages from a wide array of early modern writing about the play's many concerns; and the Applause Shakespeare Library edition (2001), with an introduction by Randall Martin and commentary by Peter Lichtenfels which explores some of the possible ways moments in the play might be performed. A selection of contextual materials covering a wider scope than Kaplan's is S. P. Cerasano's Routledge Literary Sourcebook on *William Shakespeare's 'The Merchant of Venice'* (2004).

Shakespeare's sources and some analogues for the play are reprinted in volume I of Geoffrey Bullough's magisterial *Narrative and Dramatic Sources of Shakespeare* (1958) and discussed in the relevant sections of the major editions cited above, as well as in Kenneth Muir's *Shakespeare's Sources* (1957). There are many modern reprints of Arthur Golding's 1567 translation of Ovid's *Metamorphoses*, which must have been Shakespeare's favourite book, as well as the particular translations of the Bible on which he drew.

For the play's life in the theatre, in addition to Edelman's edition, there are some outstanding studies, including John Gross's thoughtful exploration of *Shylock: Four Hundred Years in the Life of a Legend* (1992), James C. Bulman's detailed and perceptive study of selected productions in his book for the Shakespeare in Performance series (1991), and Miriam Gilbert's superb analysis of the productions in one rather important town for the Shakespeare at Stratford series (2002). Patrick Stewart gives a fascinating account of playing Shylock in *Players of Shakespeare 1*, edited by Philip Brockbank (1985). Stewart and David Suchet recount their approaches to the role in conversation with their director John Barton in Barton's *Playing Shakespeare* (1984); the video of the television programme on which the book is based is also available. Other actors have given insights into their preparation of roles in the play in the *Players of Shakespeare* collections: Sinead Cusack writes on Portia in volume 1 and Deborah Findlay on the same role in volume 3 (edited by Russell Jackson and Robert Smallwood, 1993); Ian McDiarmid on Shylock in volume 2 (same editors, 1988); Gregory Doran on Solanio in volume 3; and Christopher Luscombe on Launcelot Gobbo in volume 4 (edited by Robert Smallwood, 1998). Harley Granville-Barker's analysis of the play in his *Prefaces to Shakespeare* (2nd series, 1930) is suffused with understanding of the play in performance. Glenda Leeming's edition of Arnold Wesker's *The Merchant* (1983) provides helpful notes and commentary.

Two major stage productions were filmed for television and transferred to video or DVD: Jonathan Miller's with Sir Laurence Olivier as Shylock (directed by John Sichel, 1973; Universal Pictures, 1999) and Trevor Nunn's with Henry Goodman in the role (directed by Trevor Nunn, 2001; Metrodome Distribution, 2003), both originally for the National Theatre. The BBC TV production for its Shakespeare series with Warren Mitchell was made in 1980. The tantalizing missing film is that by Orson Welles with Welles as Shylock, nearly completed and then stolen. As I write this a film version with Al Pacino as Shylock and Jeremy Irons as Antonio is completing production. There are fine audio-recordings currently available on audiotape and CD, including Orson Welles's Mercury Theatre production of the 1930s, one in the Caedmon series from the 1960s with Hugh Griffith, a BBC radio production with Warren Mitchell and, most recently, an Arkangel recording starring Trevor Peacock.

The best places to begin reading critics' accounts of the play are probably some of the fine anthologies that have brought together what the editors see as the best writing on the play. John Wilders's 1969 volume for the Macmillan Casebook series gives a well-chosen survey of the critical material to that date, while Martin Coyle's collection for the New Casebook series (1998) adroitly gathers the best and most provocative articles informed by recent theoretical models. Harold Bloom's collection for his series of Modern Critical Interpretations (1986) is also useful and includes Freud's essay on 'The Theme of the Three Caskets', while the four essays Nigel Wood commissioned for the volume in his Theory in Practice series (1995) are all intriguing, as are a few of the best pieces in John and Ellen Macleod Mahon's *New Critical Essays* (2002). Thomas Wheeler's *'The Merchant of Venice': Critical Essays* (1991) is also very helpful. Many of the articles mentioned below are in one or more of these anthologies.

Of older criticism, perhaps the essays that continue to have most resonance in the different critical climate of today are C. L. Barber's chapter in *Shakespeare's Festive Comedy* (1959), John Russell Brown's chapter in his *Shakespeare and His Comedies* (1957) and Frank Kermode's 'The Mature Comedies' in *Early Shakespeare* (edited by John Russell Brown and Bernard Harris, 1961). W. H. Auden's 'Brothers and Others' (first printed in his *The Dyer's Hand*, 1963) is typically intriguing and quirky. Book-length studies that belong to this kind of critical tradition include Lawrence Danson's *The Harmonies of 'The Merchant of Venice'* (1978) and John Lyon's *The Merchant of Venice* (1988).

More recent work might be divided between different kinds of overlapping approaches. Marxist criticism could be represented by Kiernan Ryan's chapter 'Rereading *The Merchant of Venice*' in his *Shakespeare* (2nd edn, 1995). New Historicist criticism is demonstrated by Walter Cohen's '*The Merchant of Venice* and the Possibilities of Historical Criticism' (in Coyle) and John Drakakis's 'Historical Difference and Venetian Patriarchy' (in Coyle and in Wood). Gender and sexuality studies are best found in Karen Newman's 'Portia's Ring: Unruly Women and Structures of Exchange in *The Merchant of Venice*', Catherine Belsey's 'Love in Venice' and Alan Sinfield's 'How to Read *The Merchant of Venice* Without Being Heterosexist' (all in Coyle). Postcolonial theory is used by Kim Hall in 'Guess Who's Coming to Dinner?' (again in Coyle). Economic history is excellently demonstrated by Marc Shell in his 'The Wether and the Ewe: Verbal Usury' (in Bloom). Each of these essays cannot be constricted to a single category of modern criticism; each re-examines the play to fine effect. The most stimulating essay of the last few years may well be Stephen Orgel's 'Imagining Shylock' in his *Imagining Shakespeare* (2003).

Some contexts richly repay further exploration. James Shapiro's book on *Shakespeare and the Jews* (1996) is by far the best account and draws on much historical study of Jews in England, e.g. Cecil Roth's *A History of the Jews in England* (3rd edn, 1964), now replaced by David S. Katz's *The Jews in the History of England, 1485–1850* (1994). For perspective on the Jews of Venice, *The Jews of Early Modern Europe* (edited by Robert C. Davis and Benjamin Ravid, 2001) is particularly helpful. A modern aspect of the matter, productions of the play in Israel, is pursued by Avraham Oz in 'Transformations of Authenticity' (in Coyle). Stephen Greenblatt's 'Marlowe, Marx and Anti-Semitism' in his *Learning to Curse* (1990) explores an early modern context for the Jew onstage.

Steven Marx's *Shakespeare and the Bible* (2000) has a chapter on *The Merchant of Venice*.

Studies of early modern Venice include Frederic C. Lane's general history *Venice: A Maritime Republic* (1973), Gary Wills's *Venice: Lion City* (2001) and Stanley Chojnacki's collection on *Women and Men in Renaissance Venice* (2000). Sir John Hale's *England and the Italian Renaissance* (1954) is irreplaceable while Michele Marrapodi's collection *Shakespeare's Italy* (1997) has some fine essays on many aspects of Shakespeare's repeated use of Italian settings.

R. H. Tawney's 1925 edition of Thomas Wilson's *Discourse Upon Usury* (1572) is still important, not least for its introduction. For material on early modern economics, Norman Jones's *God and the Moneylenders* (1989) is excellent as is Sandra K. Fischer's *Econolingua: A Glossary of Coins and Economic Language in Renaissance Drama* (1985). There are perceptive essays on Shakespeare's attitudes to money, many in English, in M. T. Jones-Davies's anthology on *Shakespeare et l'argent* (1993), particularly Stanley Wells's 'Money in Shakespeare's Comedies'.

THE COMICAL HISTORY OF THE MERCHANT OF VENICE, OR OTHERWISE CALLED THE JEW OF VENICE

The Characters in the Play

The DUKE of Venice
ANTONIO, a merchant of Venice
BASSANIO, his friend, suitor of Portia
GRATIANO
SALERIO } friends of Antonio and Bassanio
SOLANIO
LORENZO, in love with Jessica
LEONARDO, servant of Bassanio

SHYLOCK, a Jew of Venice
JESSICA, his daughter
TUBAL, a Jew of Venice, Shylock's friend
LAUNCELOT Gobbo, servant of Shylock
Old GOBBO, father of Launcelot

PORTIA, the Lady of Belmont
NERISSA, Portia's waiting-woman
The Prince of MOROCCO } suitors of Portia
The Prince of ARRAGON
BALTHASAR } servants of Portia
STEPHANO

SERVINGMAN
MESSENGER

Antonio's MAN
CLERK

Magnificoes of Venice, officers of the Court of Justice, a
gaoler, musicians, servants and other attendants

For Salarino, see p. 105.

ANTONIO

In sooth I know not why I am so sad.
It wearies me, you say it wearies you;
But how I caught it, found it, or came by it,
What stuff 'tis made of, whereof it is born,
I am to learn;
And such a want-wit sadness makes of me
That I have much ado to know myself.

SALERIO

Your mind is tossing on the ocean,
There where your argosies with portly sail,
Like signors and rich burghers on the flood,   10
Or as it were the pageants of the sea,
Do overpeer the petty traffickers
That curtsy to them, do them reverence,
As they fly by them with their woven wings.

SOLANIO

Believe me, sir, had I such venture forth,
The better part of my affections would
Be with my hopes abroad. I should be still
Plucking the grass to know where sits the wind,
Peering in maps for ports and piers and roads,
And every object that might make me fear   20

Misfortune to my ventures, out of doubt
Would make me sad.

SALERIO   My wind cooling my broth
Would blow me to an ague when I thought
What harm a wind too great might do at sea.
I should not see the sandy hour-glass run
But I should think of shallows and of flats,
And see my wealthy Andrew docked in sand,
Vailing her high-top lower than her ribs
To kiss her burial. Should I go to church
30   And see the holy edifice of stone
And not bethink me straight of dangerous rocks,
Which touching but my gentle vessel's side
Would scatter all her spices on the stream,
Enrobe the roaring waters with my silks,
And in a word, but even now worth this,
And now worth nothing? Shall I have the thought
To think on this, and shall I lack the thought
That such a thing bechanced would make me sad?
But tell not me; I know Antonio
40   Is sad to think upon his merchandise.

ANTONIO
Believe me, no. I thank my fortune for it
My ventures are not in one bottom trusted,
Nor to one place; nor is my whole estate
Upon the fortune of this present year.
Therefore my merchandise makes me not sad.

SOLANIO
Why then you are in love.

ANTONIO   Fie, fie!

SOLANIO
Not in love neither? Then let us say you are sad
Because you are not merry; and 'twere as easy
For you to laugh and leap, and say you are merry

Because you are not sad. Now by two-headed Janus,   50
Nature hath framed strange fellows in her time:
Some that will evermore peep through their eyes
And laugh like parrots at a bagpiper,
And other of such vinegar aspect
That they'll not show their teeth in way of smile
Though Nestor swear the jest be laughable.
    Enter Bassanio, Lorenzo, and Gratiano
Here comes Bassanio your most noble kinsman,
Gratiano, and Lorenzo. Fare ye well;
We leave you now with better company.

SALERIO

I would have stayed till I had made you merry,   60
If worthier friends had not prevented me.

ANTONIO

Your worth is very dear in my regard.
I take it your own business calls on you,
And you embrace th'occasion to depart.

SALERIO

Good morrow, my good lords.

BASSANIO

Good signors both, when shall we laugh? Say, when?
You grow exceeding strange. Must it be so?

SALERIO

We'll make our leisures to attend on yours.
                    Exeunt Salerio and Solanio

LORENZO

My Lord Bassanio, since you have found Antonio,
We two will leave you; but at dinner-time   70
I pray you have in mind where we must meet.

BASSANIO

I will not fail you.

GRATIANO

You look not well, Signor Antonio.

You have too much respect upon the world;
They lose it that do buy it with much care.
Believe me, you are marvellously changed.

ANTONIO

I hold the world but as the world, Gratiano,
A stage where every man must play a part,
And mine a sad one.

GRATIANO   Let me play the fool;
80   With mirth and laughter let old wrinkles come,
And let my liver rather heat with wine
Than my heart cool with mortifying groans.
Why should a man whose blood is warm within
Sit, like his grandsire cut in alabaster?
Sleep when he wakes? And creep into the jaundice
By being peevish? I tell thee what, Antonio,
I love thee, and 'tis my love that speaks:
There are a sort of men whose visages
Do cream and mantle like a standing pond,
90   And do a wilful stillness entertain
With purpose to be dressed in an opinion
Of wisdom, gravity, profound conceit,
As who should say, 'I am Sir Oracle,
And when I ope my lips, let no dog bark.'
O my Antonio, I do know of these
That therefore only are reputed wise
For saying nothing, when I am very sure
If they should speak, would almost damn those ears,
Which hearing them would call their brothers fools.
100   I'll tell thee more of this another time.
But fish not with this melancholy bait
For this fool gudgeon, this opinion.
Come, good Lorenzo. Fare ye well awhile;
I'll end my exhortation after dinner.

LORENZO

    Well, we will leave you then till dinner-time.

    I must be one of these same dumb wise men,

    For Gratiano never lets me speak.

GRATIANO

    Well, keep me company but two years more,

    Thou shalt not know the sound of thine own tongue.

ANTONIO

    Fare you well; I'll grow a talker for this gear.   110

GRATIANO

    Thanks i'faith; for silence is only commendable

    In a neat's tongue dried and a maid not vendible.

                   Exeunt Gratiano and Lorenzo

ANTONIO Is that anything now?

BASSANIO Gratiano speaks an infinite deal of nothing, more than any man in all Venice. His reasons are as two grains of wheat hid in two bushels of chaff: you shall seek all day ere you find them, and when you have them they are not worth the search.

ANTONIO

    Well, tell me now what lady is the same

    To whom you swore a secret pilgrimage,   120

    That you today promised to tell me of.

BASSANIO

    'Tis not unknown to you, Antonio,

    How much I have disabled mine estate

    By something showing a more swelling port

    Than my faint means would grant continuance.

    Nor do I now make moan to be abridged

    From such a noble rate; but my chief care

    Is to come fairly off from the great debts

    Wherein my time, something too prodigal,

    Hath left me gaged. To you, Antonio,   130

    I owe the most in money and in love,

And from your love I have a warranty
To unburden all my plots and purposes
How to get clear of all the debts I owe.

ANTONIO

I pray you, good Bassanio, let me know it,
And if it stand as you yourself still do,
Within the eye of honour, be assured
My purse, my person, my extremest means
Lie all unlocked to your occasions.

BASSANIO

140   In my schooldays, when I had lost one shaft,
I shot his fellow of the self-same flight
The self-same way, with more advisèd watch,
To find the other forth; and by adventuring both
I oft found both. I urge this childhood proof
Because what follows is pure innocence.
I owe you much, and like a wilful youth,
That which I owe is lost; but if you please
To shoot another arrow that self way
Which you did shoot the first, I do not doubt,
150   As I will watch the aim, or to find both
Or bring your latter hazard back again
And thankfully rest debtor for the first.

ANTONIO

You know me well, and herein spend but time
To wind about my love with circumstance;
And out of doubt you do me now more wrong
In making question of my uttermost
Than if you had made waste of all I have.
Then do but say to me what I should do
That in your knowledge may by me be done,
160   And I am prest unto it. Therefore speak.

BASSANIO

In Belmont is a lady richly left,

And she is fair, and, fairer than that word,
Of wondrous virtues. Sometimes from her eyes
I did receive fair speechless messages.
Her name is Portia, nothing undervalued
To Cato's daughter, Brutus' Portia;
Nor is the wide world ignorant of her worth,
For the four winds blow in from every coast
Renownèd suitors, and her sunny locks
Hang on her temples like a golden fleece,   170
Which makes her seat of Belmont Colchos' strond,
And many Jasons come in quest of her.
O my Antonio, had I but the means
To hold a rival place with one of them,
I have a mind presages me such thrift
That I should questionless be fortunate.

ANTONIO
Thou know'st that all my fortunes are at sea,
Neither have I money, nor commodity
To raise a present sum. Therefore go forth;
Try what my credit can in Venice do,   180
That shall be racked even to the uttermost
To furnish thee to Belmont, to fair Portia.
Go presently inquire, and so will I,
Where money is; and I no question make
To have it of my trust or for my sake.   *Exeunt*

Enter Portia with her waiting-woman, Nerissa   1.2

PORTIA By my troth, Nerissa, my little body is aweary of
    this great world.
NERISSA You would be, sweet madam, if your miseries
    were in the same abundance as your good fortunes are;
    and yet for aught I see, they are as sick that surfeit with
    too much as they that starve with nothing. It is no mean

happiness, therefore, to be seated in the mean; superfluity comes sooner by white hairs, but competency lives
longer.

10 PORTIA Good sentences, and well pronounced.

NERISSA They would be better if well followed.

PORTIA If to do were as easy as to know what were good
to do, chapels had been churches, and poor men's
cottages princes' palaces. It is a good divine that follows
his own instructions. I can easier teach twenty what were
good to be done than to be one of the twenty to follow
mine own teaching. The brain may devise laws for the
blood, but a hot temper leaps o'er a cold decree, such a
hare is madness the youth to skip o'er the meshes of good
20 counsel the cripple. But this reasoning is not in the
fashion to choose me a husband. O me, the word
'choose'! I may neither choose who I would nor refuse
who I dislike, so is the will of a living daughter curbed
by the will of a dead father. Is it not hard, Nerissa, that I
cannot choose one, nor refuse none?

NERISSA Your father was ever virtuous, and holy men at
their death have good inspirations. Therefore the lottery
that he hath devised in these three chests of gold, silver,
and lead, whereof who chooses his meaning chooses you,
30 will no doubt never be chosen by any rightly but one
who you shall rightly love. But what warmth is there in
your affection towards any of these princely suitors that
are already come?

PORTIA I pray thee overname them, and as thou namest
them I will describe them, and according to my description level at my affection.

NERISSA First, there is the Neapolitan prince.

PORTIA Ay, that's a colt indeed, for he doth nothing but
talk of his horse, and he makes it a great appropriation to
40 his own good parts that he can shoe him himself. I am

much afeard my lady his mother played false with a
smith.

NERISSA Then is there the County Palatine.

PORTIA He doth nothing but frown, as who should say,
'An you will not have me, choose.' He hears merry tales
and smiles not. I fear he will prove the weeping philosopher when he grows old, being so full of unmannerly
sadness in his youth. I had rather be married to a death's-
head with a bone in his mouth than to either of these.
God defend me from these two!   50

NERISSA How say you by the French lord, Monsieur Le
Bon?

PORTIA God made him and therefore let him pass for a
man. In truth, I know it is a sin to be a mocker, but he,
why he hath a horse better than the Neapolitan's, a better
bad habit of frowning than the Count Palatine; he is
every man in no man. If a throstle sing, he falls straight
a-capering; he will fence with his own shadow. If I
should marry him, I should marry twenty husbands. If
he would despise me, I would forgive him, for if he love   60
me to madness, I shall never requite him.

NERISSA What say you then to Falconbridge, the young
baron of England?

PORTIA You know I say nothing to him, for he understands not me, nor I him. He hath neither Latin, French,
nor Italian, and you will come into the court and swear
that I have a poor pennyworth in the English. He is a
proper man's picture, but alas, who can converse with a
dumb-show? How oddly he is suited! I think he bought
his doublet in Italy, his round hose in France, his bonnet   70
in Germany, and his behaviour everywhere.

NERISSA What think you of the Scottish lord, his neighbour?

PORTIA That he hath a neighbourly charity in him, for he

borrowed a box of the ear of the Englishman and swore
he would pay him again when he was able. I think the
Frenchman became his surety and sealed under for
another.

NERISSA How like you the young German, the Duke of
Saxony's nephew?

PORTIA Very vilely in the morning when he is sober and
most vilely in the afternoon when he is drunk. When he
is best he is a little worse than a man, and when he is
worst he is little better than a beast. An the worst fall
that ever fell, I hope I shall make shift to go without him.

NERISSA If he should offer to choose, and choose the right
casket, you should refuse to perform your father's will
if you should refuse to accept him.

PORTIA Therefore, for fear of the worst, I pray thee set a
deep glass of Rhenish wine on the contrary casket, for if
the devil be within and that temptation without, I know
he will choose it. I will do anything, Nerissa, ere I will be
married to a sponge.

NERISSA You need not fear, lady, the having any of these
lords. They have acquainted me with their determina-
tions, which is indeed to return to their home and to
trouble you with no more suit, unless you may be won
by some other sort than your father's imposition, depending on the caskets.

PORTIA If I live to be as old as Sibylla, I will die as chaste
as Diana unless I be obtained by the manner of my
father's will. I am glad this parcel of wooers are so
reasonable, for there is not one among them but I dote
on his very absence, and I pray God grant them a fair
departure.

NERISSA Do you not remember, lady, in your father's
time, a Venetian, a scholar and a soldier, that came
hither in company of the Marquis of Montferrat?

PORTIA Yes, yes, it was Bassanio, as I think, so was he
called.   110

NERISSA True, madam. He, of all the men that ever my
foolish eyes looked upon, was the best deserving a fair
lady.

PORTIA I remember him well, and I remember him
worthy of thy praise.

    Enter a Servingman

How now, what news?

SERVINGMAN The four strangers seek for you, madam, to
take their leave, and there is a forerunner come from a
fifth, the Prince of Morocco, who brings word the Prince
his master will be here tonight.   120

PORTIA If I could bid the fifth welcome with so good
heart as I can bid the other four farewell, I should be
glad of his approach. If he have the condition of a saint
and the complexion of a devil, I had rather he should
shrive me than wive me. Come, Nerissa. Sirrah, go
before. Whiles we shut the gate upon one wooer, another
knocks at the door.   *Exeunt*

    Enter Bassanio with Shylock the Jew   I.3

SHYLOCK Three thousand ducats, well.

BASSANIO Ay, sir, for three months.

SHYLOCK For three months, well.

BASSANIO For the which, as I told you, Antonio shall be
bound.

SHYLOCK Antonio shall become bound, well.

BASSANIO May you stead me? Will you pleasure me?
Shall I know your answer?

SHYLOCK Three thousand ducats for three months, and
Antonio bound.   10

BASSANIO Your answer to that.

SHYLOCK Antonio is a good man.

BASSANIO Have you heard any imputation to the contrary?

SHYLOCK Ho no, no, no, no! My meaning in saying he is a good man is to have you understand me that he is sufficient. Yet his means are in supposition. He hath an argosy bound to Tripolis, another to the Indies; I understand, moreover, upon the Rialto, he hath a third at Mexico, a fourth for England, and other ventures he hath squandered abroad. But ships are but boards, sailors but men; there be land rats and water rats, water thieves and land thieves, I mean pirates; and then there is the peril of waters, winds, and rocks. The man is, notwithstanding, sufficient. Three thousand ducats; I think I may take his bond.

BASSANIO Be assured you may.

SHYLOCK I will be assured I may; and that I may be assured, I will bethink me. May I speak with Antonio?

BASSANIO If it please you to dine with us.

SHYLOCK Yes, to smell pork, to eat of the habitation which your prophet the Nazarite conjured the devil into. I will buy with you, sell with you, talk with you, walk with you, and so following; but I will not eat with you, drink with you, nor pray with you. What news on the Rialto? Who is he comes here?

Enter Antonio

BASSANIO
This is Signor Antonio.

SHYLOCK (*aside*)
How like a fawning publican he looks.
I hate him for he is a Christian;
But more, for that in low simplicity
He lends out money gratis and brings down
The rate of usance here with us in Venice.

If I can catch him once upon the hip,
I will feed fat the ancient grudge I bear him.
He hates our sacred nation and he rails
Even there where merchants most do congregate
On me, my bargains, and my well-won thrift,
Which he calls interest. Cursèd be my tribe
If I forgive him.

BASSANIO   Shylock, do you hear?

SHYLOCK

I am debating of my present store,   50
And by the near guess of my memory
I cannot instantly raise up the gross
Of full three thousand ducats. What of that?
Tubal, a wealthy Hebrew of my tribe,
Will furnish me. But soft, how many months
Do you desire? (*To Antonio*) Rest you fair, good signor!
Your worship was the last man in our mouths.

ANTONIO

Shylock, albeit I neither lend nor borrow
By taking nor by giving of excess,
Yet to supply the ripe wants of my friend,   60
I'll break a custom. (*To Bassanio*) Is he yet possessed
How much ye would?

SHYLOCK   Ay, ay, three thousand ducats.

ANTONIO

And for three months.

SHYLOCK

I had forgot – three months, you told me so.
Well then, your bond. And let me see; but hear you,
Methoughts you said you neither lend nor borrow
Upon advantage.

ANTONIO   I do never use it.

SHYLOCK

When Jacob grazed his uncle Laban's sheep –

This Jacob from our holy Abram was,
70   As his wise mother wrought in his behalf,
The third possessor; ay, he was the third –

ANTONIO
And what of him? Did he take interest?

SHYLOCK
No, not take interest, not as you would say
Directly interest. Mark what Jacob did:
When Laban and himself were compromised
That all the eanlings which were streaked and pied
Should fall as Jacob's hire, the ewes being rank,
In end of autumn turnèd to the rams;
And when the work of generation was
80   Between these woolly breeders in the act,
The skilful shepherd peeled me certain wands,
And in the doing of the deed of kind
He stuck them up before the fulsome ewes,
Who then conceiving, did in eaning time
Fall parti-coloured lambs, and those were Jacob's.
This was a way to thrive, and he was blest,
And thrift is blessing if men steal it not.

ANTONIO
This was a venture, sir, that Jacob served for,
A thing not in his power to bring to pass,
90   But swayed and fashioned by the hand of heaven.
Was this inserted to make interest good?
Or is your gold and silver ewes and rams?

SHYLOCK
I cannot tell, I make it breed as fast.
But note me, signor –

ANTONIO   Mark you this, Bassanio,
The devil can cite Scripture for his purpose.
An evil soul producing holy witness
Is like a villain with a smiling cheek,

A goodly apple rotten at the heart.
O what a goodly outside falsehood hath!

SHYLOCK

Three thousand ducats, 'tis a good round sum.   100
Three months from twelve, then let me see, the rate . . .

ANTONIO

Well, Shylock, shall we be beholding to you?

SHYLOCK

Signor Antonio, many a time and oft
In the Rialto you have rated me
About my moneys and my usances.
Still have I borne it with a patient shrug,
For sufferance is the badge of all our tribe.
You call me misbeliever, cut-throat dog,
And spit upon my Jewish gaberdine,
And all for use of that which is mine own.   110
Well then, it now appears you need my help.
Go to then. You come to me and you say,
'Shylock, we would have moneys,' you say so,
You, that did void your rheum upon my beard
And foot me as you spurn a stranger cur
Over your threshold, moneys is your suit.
What should I say to you? Should I not say,
'Hath a dog money? Is it possible
A cur can lend three thousand ducats?' Or
Shall I bend low, and in a bondman's key,   120
With bated breath and whispering humbleness,
Say this:
'Fair sir, you spat on me on Wednesday last,
You spurned me such a day, another time
You called me dog, and for these courtesies
I'll lend you thus much moneys'?

ANTONIO

I am as like to call thee so again,

To spit on thee again, to spurn thee too.
If thou wilt lend this money, lend it not
130   As to thy friends, for when did friendship take
A breed of barren metal of his friend?
But lend it rather to thine enemy,
Who if he break, thou mayst with better face
Exact the penalty.

SHYLOCK   Why look you, how you storm!
I would be friends with you and have your love,
Forget the shames that you have stained me with,
Supply your present wants, and take no doit
Of usance for my moneys, and you'll not hear me.
This is kind I offer.

BASSANIO
140   This were kindness.

SHYLOCK   This kindness will I show.
Go with me to a notary, seal me there
Your single bond, and, in a merry sport,
If you repay me not on such a day,
In such a place, such sum or sums as are
Expressed in the condition, let the forfeit
Be nominated for an equal pound
Of your fair flesh, to be cut off and taken
In what part of your body pleaseth me.

ANTONIO
Content, in faith. I'll seal to such a bond
150   And say there is much kindness in the Jew.

BASSANIO
You shall not seal to such a bond for me;
I'll rather dwell in my necessity.

ANTONIO
Why fear not, man; I will not forfeit it.
Within these two months – that's a month before
This bond expires – I do expect return

Of thrice three times the value of this bond.

SHYLOCK

O father Abram, what these Christians are,
Whose own hard dealings teaches them suspect
The thoughts of others! Pray you tell me this:
If he should break his day, what should I gain   160
By the exaction of the forfeiture?
A pound of man's flesh taken from a man
Is not so estimable, profitable neither,
As flesh of muttons, beefs, or goats. I say
To buy his favour I extend this friendship.
If he will take it, so; if not, adieu.
And for my love I pray you wrong me not.

ANTONIO

Yes, Shylock, I will seal unto this bond.

SHYLOCK

Then meet me forthwith at the notary's;
Give him direction for this merry bond,   170
And I will go and purse the ducats straight,
See to my house, left in the fearful guard
Of an unthrifty knave, and presently
I'll be with you.   *Exit*

ANTONIO   Hie thee, gentle Jew.
The Hebrew will turn Christian; he grows kind.

BASSANIO

I like not fair terms and a villain's mind.

ANTONIO

Come on. In this there can be no dismay;
My ships come home a month before the day. *Exeunt*

*

II.I   *Flourish of cornets. Enter the Prince of Morocco, a*
          tawny Moor all in white, and three or four followers
          accordingly, with Portia, Nerissa, and their train

MOROCCO

Mislike me not for my complexion,
The shadowed livery of the burnished sun,
To whom I am a neighbour and near bred.
Bring me the fairest creature northward born,
Where Phoebus' fire scarce thaws the icicles,
And let us make incision for your love
To prove whose blood is reddest, his or mine.
I tell thee, lady, this aspect of mine
Hath feared the valiant. By my love I swear,
10   The best-regarded virgins of our clime
Have loved it too. I would not change this hue,
Except to steal your thoughts, my gentle queen.

PORTIA

In terms of choice I am not solely led
By nice direction of a maiden's eyes.
Besides, the lott'ry of my destiny
Bars me the right of voluntary choosing.
But if my father had not scanted me,
And hedged me by his wit to yield myself
His wife who wins me by that means I told you,
20   Yourself, renownèd Prince, then stood as fair
As any comer I have looked on yet
For my affection.

MOROCCO   Even for that I thank you.
Therefore I pray you lead me to the caskets
To try my fortune. By this scimitar
That slew the Sophy and a Persian prince
That won three fields of Sultan Solyman,
I would o'erstare the sternest eyes that look,
Outbrave the heart most daring on the earth,

Pluck the young sucking cubs from the she-bear,
Yea, mock the lion when 'a roars for prey,   30
To win thee, lady. But alas the while,
If Hercules and Lichas play at dice
Which is the better man, the greater throw
May turn by fortune from the weaker hand.
So is Alcides beaten by his page,
And so may I, blind Fortune leading me,
Miss that which one unworthier may attain,
And die with grieving.

PORTIA   You must take your chance,
And either not attempt to choose at all
Or swear before you choose, if you choose wrong   40
Never to speak to lady afterward
In way of marriage. Therefore be advised.

MOROCCO
Nor will not. Come, bring me unto my chance.

PORTIA
First, forward to the temple; after dinner
Your hazard shall be made.

MOROCCO   Good fortune then,
To make me blest or cursèd'st among men!

                         Flourish of cornets. Exeunt

Enter Launcelot Gobbo, alone   **II.2**

LAUNCELOT Certainly my conscience will serve me to run
from this Jew my master. The fiend is at mine elbow and
tempts me, saying to me, 'Gobbo, Launcelot Gobbo,
good Launcelot,' or 'Good Gobbo,' or 'Good Launcelot
Gobbo, use your legs, take the start, run away.' My conscience says, 'No, take heed, honest Launcelot, take
heed, honest Gobbo,' or as aforesaid, 'Honest Launcelot
Gobbo, do not run, scorn running with thy heels.' Well,

the most courageous fiend bids me pack. 'Fia!' says the
fiend; 'Away!' says the fiend. 'For the heavens, rouse up a
brave mind,' says the fiend, 'and run.' Well, my conscience hanging about the neck of my heart says very
wisely to me, 'My honest friend Launcelot', being an
honest man's son or rather an honest woman's son, for
indeed my father did something smack, something grow
to, he had a kind of taste – well, my conscience says,
'Launcelot, budge not.' 'Budge,' says the fiend. 'Budge
not,' says my conscience. 'Conscience,' say I, 'you counsel well.' 'Fiend,' say I, 'you counsel well.' To be ruled
by my conscience, I should stay with the Jew my master
who, God bless the mark, is a kind of devil; and to run
away from the Jew, I should be ruled by the fiend, who,
saving your reverence, is the devil himself. Certainly the
Jew is the very devil incarnation; and in my conscience,
my conscience is but a kind of hard conscience to offer to
counsel me to stay with the Jew. The fiend gives the
more friendly counsel. I will run, fiend; my heels are at
your commandment; I will run.

Enter Old Gobbo with a basket

GOBBO Master young man, you I pray you, which is the
way to Master Jew's?

LAUNCELOT (*aside*) O heavens, this is my true-begotten
father who, being more than sand-blind, high-gravel-
blind, knows me not. I will try confusions with him.

GOBBO Master young gentleman, I pray you which is the
way to Master Jew's?

LAUNCELOT Turn up on your right hand at the next turning, but at the next turning of all, on your left, marry, at
the very next turning turn of no hand, but turn down
indirectly to the Jew's house.

GOBBO By God's sonties, 'twill be a hard way to hit! Can
you tell me whether one Launcelot that dwells with him,
dwell with him or no?

LAUNCELOT Talk you of young Master Launcelot?
   (aside) Mark me now, now will I raise the waters. – Talk
   you of young Master Launcelot?

GOBBO No master, sir, but a poor man's son. His father,
   though I say't, is an honest exceeding poor man and,
   God be thanked, well to live.

LAUNCELOT Well, let his father be what 'a will, we talk of
   young Master Launcelot.   50

GOBBO Your worship's friend, and Launcelot, sir.

LAUNCELOT But I pray you, ergo old man, ergo I beseech
   you, talk you of young Master Launcelot.

GOBBO Of Launcelot, an't please your mastership.

LAUNCELOT Ergo, Master Launcelot. Talk not of Master
   Launcelot, father, for the young gentleman, according to
   Fates and Destinies and such odd sayings, the Sisters
   Three and such branches of learning, is indeed deceased,
   or as you would say in plain terms, gone to heaven.

GOBBO Marry, God forbid! The boy was the very staff of   60
   my age, my very prop.

LAUNCELOT Do I look like a cudgel or a hovel-post, a
   staff or a prop? Do you know me, father?

GOBBO Alack the day, I know you not, young gentleman!
   But I pray you tell me, is my boy, God rest his soul,
   alive or dead?

LAUNCELOT Do you not know me, father?

GOBBO Alack, sir, I am sand-blind! I know you not.

LAUNCELOT Nay, indeed if you had your eyes you might
   fail of the knowing me; it is a wise father that knows his   70
   own child. Well, old man, I will tell you news of your
   son. *(He kneels)* Give me your blessing. Truth will come
   to light; murder cannot be hid long – a man's son may,
   but in the end truth will out.

GOBBO Pray you, sir, stand up. I am sure you are not
   Launcelot my boy.

LAUNCELOT Pray you let's have no more fooling about it, but give me your blessing. I am Launcelot, your boy that was, your son that is, your child that shall be.

80 GOBBO I cannot think you are my son.

LAUNCELOT I know not what I shall think of that; but I am Launcelot, the Jew's man, and I am sure Margery your wife is my mother.

GOBBO Her name is Margery indeed. I'll be sworn, if thou be Launcelot thou art mine own flesh and blood. Lord worshipped might he be, what a beard hast thou got! Thou hast got more hair on thy chin than Dobbin my fill-horse has on his tail.

LAUNCELOT It should seem then that Dobbin's tail grows
90 backward. I am sure he had more hair on his tail than I have on my face when I last saw him.

GOBBO Lord, how art thou changed! How dost thou and thy master agree? I have brought him a present. How 'gree you now?

LAUNCELOT Well, well; but for mine own part, as I have set up my rest to run away, so I will not rest till I have run some ground. My master's a very Jew. Give him a present? Give him a halter! I am famished in his service; you may tell every finger I have with my ribs. Father, I
100 am glad you are come. Give me your present to one Master Bassanio, who indeed gives rare new liveries. If I serve not him, I will run as far as God has any ground. O rare fortune, here comes the man! To him, father, for I am a Jew if I serve the Jew any longer.

Enter Bassanio, with Leonardo and a follower or two

BASSANIO You may do so, but let it be so hasted that supper be ready at the farthest by five of the clock. See these letters delivered, put the liveries to making, and desire Gratiano to come anon to my lodging.

Exit one of his men

LAUNCELOT To him, father!

GOBBO God bless your worship!   110

BASSANIO Gramercy. Wouldst thou aught with me?

GOBBO Here's my son, sir, a poor boy . . .

LAUNCELOT Not a poor boy, sir, but the rich Jew's man
    that would, sir, as my father shall specify . . .

GOBBO He hath a great infection, sir, as one would say,
    to serve . . .

LAUNCELOT Indeed, the short and the long is, I serve the
    Jew, and have a desire, as my father shall specify . . .

GOBBO His master and he, saving your worship's rever-
    ence, are scarce cater-cousins.   120

LAUNCELOT To be brief, the very truth is that the Jew
    having done me wrong doth cause me, as my father,
    being I hope an old man, shall frutify unto you . . .

GOBBO I have here a dish of doves that I would bestow
    upon your worship, and my suit is . . .

LAUNCELOT In very brief, the suit is impertinent to
    myself, as your worship shall know by this honest old
    man, and though I say it, though old man, yet poor man,
    my father . . .

BASSANIO One speak for both. What would you?   130

LAUNCELOT Serve you, sir.

GOBBO That is the very defect of the matter, sir.

BASSANIO
    I know thee well, thou hast obtained thy suit.
    Shylock thy master spoke with me this day,
    And hath preferred thee, if it be preferment
    To leave a rich Jew's service to become
    The follower of so poor a gentleman.

LAUNCELOT The old proverb is very well parted between
    my master Shylock and you, sir. You have the grace of
    God, sir, and he hath enough.   140

BASSANIO

Thou speak'st it well. Go, father, with thy son;
Take leave of thy old master and inquire
My lodging out. (*To a servant*) Give him a livery
More guarded than his fellows'. See it done.

LAUNCELOT Father, in. I cannot get a service, no! I have
ne'er a tongue in my head, well! (*He looks at his palm*) If
any man in Italy have a fairer table which doth offer to
swear upon a book, I shall have good fortune! Go to,
here's a simple line of life. Here's a small trifle of wives!

150 Alas, fifteen wives is nothing; eleven widows and nine
maids is a simple coming-in for one man. And then to
scape drowning thrice, and to be in peril of my life with
the edge of a feather-bed! Here are simple scapes. Well,
if Fortune be a woman, she's a good wench for this gear.
Father, come. I'll take my leave of the Jew in the twinkling.   *Exit Launcelot, with Old Gobbo*

BASSANIO

I pray thee, good Leonardo, think on this.
These things being bought and orderly bestowed,
Return in haste, for I do feast tonight

160 My best-esteemed acquaintance. Hie thee, go.

LEONARDO

My best endeavours shall be done herein.

Enter Gratiano

GRATIANO

Where's your master?

LEONARDO   Yonder, sir, he walks.   *Exit*

GRATIANO

Signor Bassanio!

BASSANIO

Gratiano!

GRATIANO

I have suit to you.

BASSANIO   You have obtained it.

GRATIANO
You must not deny me. I must go with you to Belmont.

BASSANIO
Why then you must. But hear thee, Gratiano:
Thou art too wild, too rude and bold of voice,
Parts that become thee happily enough
And in such eyes as ours appear not faults,   170
But where thou art not known, why there they show
Something too liberal. Pray thee take pain
To allay with some cold drops of modesty
Thy skipping spirit, lest through thy wild behaviour
I be misconstered in the place I go to,
And lose my hopes.

GRATIANO   Signor Bassanio, hear me:
If I do not put on a sober habit,
Talk with respect, and swear but now and then,
Wear prayer books in my pocket, look demurely,
Nay more, while grace is saying hood mine eyes   180
Thus with my hat, and sigh and say amen,
Use all the observance of civility
Like one well studied in a sad ostent
To please his grandam, never trust me more.

BASSANIO
Well, we shall see your bearing.

GRATIANO
Nay, but I bar tonight. You shall not gauge me
By what we do tonight.

BASSANIO   No, that were pity.
I would entreat you rather to put on
Your boldest suit of mirth, for we have friends
That purpose merriment. But fare you well;   190
I have some business.

GRATIANO

And I must to Lorenzo and the rest,
But we will visit you at supper-time.   *Exeunt*

II.3   *Enter Jessica and Launcelot the Clown*

JESSICA

I am sorry thou wilt leave my father so.
Our house is hell, and thou a merry devil
Didst rob it of some taste of tediousness.
But fare thee well, there is a ducat for thee.
And, Launcelot, soon at supper shalt thou see
Lorenzo, who is thy new master's guest.
Give him this letter; do it secretly.
And so farewell; I would not have my father
See me in talk with thee.

10 LAUNCELOT Adieu! Tears exhibit my tongue. Most beautiful pagan, most sweet Jew! If a Christian did not play the knave and get thee, I am much deceived. But adieu. These foolish drops do something drown my manly spirit. Adieu!

JESSICA

Farewell, good Launcelot.   *Exit Launcelot*
Alack, what heinous sin is it in me
To be ashamed to be my father's child.
But though I am a daughter to his blood,
I am not to his manners. O Lorenzo,
20 If thou keep promise, I shall end this strife,
Become a Christian and thy loving wife.

II.4   *Enter Gratiano, Lorenzo, Salerio, and Solanio*

LORENZO

Nay, we will slink away in supper-time,

Disguise us at my lodging, and return
All in an hour.

GRATIANO

We have not made good preparation.

SALERIO

We have not spoke us yet of torchbearers.

SOLANIO

'Tis vile, unless it may be quaintly ordered,
And better in my mind not undertook.

LORENZO

'Tis now but four of clock. We have two hours
To furnish us.

Enter Launcelot with a letter
           Friend Launcelot, what's the news?

LAUNCELOT An it shall please you to break up this, it   10
shall seem to signify.

LORENZO

I know the hand. In faith, 'tis a fair hand,
And whiter than the paper it writ on
Is the fair hand that writ.

GRATIANO   Love-news, in faith!

LAUNCELOT By your leave, sir.

LORENZO Whither goest thou?

LAUNCELOT Marry, sir, to bid my old master the Jew to
sup tonight with my new master the Christian.

LORENZO

Hold here, take this. (*Gives money*) Tell gentle Jessica
I will not fail her. Speak it privately.   *Exit Launcelot*   20
Go, gentlemen;
Will you prepare you for this masque tonight?
I am provided of a torchbearer.

SALERIO

Ay marry, I'll be gone about it straight.

SOLANIO

And so will I.

LORENZO   Meet me and Gratiano
At Gratiano's lodging some hour hence.

SALERIO
'Tis good we do so.   *Exit with Solanio*

GRATIANO
Was not that letter from fair Jessica?

LORENZO
I must needs tell thee all. She hath directed
30   How I shall take her from her father's house,
What gold and jewels she is furnished with,
What page's suit she hath in readiness.
If e'er the Jew her father come to heaven,
It will be for his gentle daughter's sake;
And never dare misfortune cross her foot,
Unless she do it under this excuse,
That she is issue to a faithless Jew.
Come, go with me; peruse this as thou goest.
Fair Jessica shall be my torchbearer. *Exit with Gratiano*

II.5   *Enter Shylock the Jew and Launcelot, his man that
            was, the Clown*

SHYLOCK
Well, thou shalt see, thy eyes shall be thy judge,
The difference of old Shylock and Bassanio . . .
What, Jessica! Thou shalt not gormandize
As thou hast done with me . . . What, Jessica! . . .
And sleep, and snore, and rend apparel out . . .
Why, Jessica, I say!

LAUNCELOT   Why, Jessica!

SHYLOCK
Who bids thee call? I do not bid thee call.

LAUNCELOT Your worship was wont to tell me I could do
nothing without bidding.

Enter Jessica

JESSICA

    Call you? What is your will?   10

SHYLOCK

    I am bid forth to supper, Jessica.

    There are my keys. But wherefore should I go?

    I am not bid for love, they flatter me,

    But yet I'll go in hate to feed upon

    The prodigal Christian. Jessica my girl,

    Look to my house. I am right loath to go.

    There is some ill a-brewing towards my rest,

    For I did dream of money bags tonight.

LAUNCELOT I beseech you, sir, go. My young master

    doth expect your reproach.   20

SHYLOCK So do I his.

LAUNCELOT And they have conspired together. I will not

    say you shall see a masque, but if you do, then it was not

    for nothing that my nose fell a-bleeding on Black Mon-

    day last at six o'clock i'th'morning, falling out that year

    on Ash Wednesday was four year in th'afternoon.

SHYLOCK

    What, are there masques? Hear you me, Jessica:

    Lock up my doors; and when you hear the drum

    And the vile squealing of the wry-necked fife,

    Clamber not you up to the casements then,   30

    Nor thrust your head into the public street

    To gaze on Christian fools with varnished faces;

    But stop my house's ears, I mean my casements;

    Let not the sound of shallow foppery enter

    My sober house. By Jacob's staff I swear

    I have no mind of feasting forth tonight,

    But I will go. Go you before me, sirrah.

    Say I will come.

LAUNCELOT   I will go before, sir.

Mistress, look out at window for all this:
40   There will come a Christian by
      Will be worth a Jewess' eye.   *Exit*

SHYLOCK
    What says that fool of Hagar's offspring, ha?

JESSICA
    His words were 'Farewell, mistress', nothing else.

SHYLOCK
    The patch is kind enough, but a huge feeder,
    Snail-slow in profit, and he sleeps by day
    More than the wildcat. Drones hive not with me;
    Therefore I part with him, and part with him
    To one that I would have him help to waste
    His borrowed purse. Well, Jessica, go in.
50   Perhaps I will return immediately.
    Do as I bid you; shut doors after you.
    Fast bind, fast find,
    A proverb never stale in thrifty mind.   *Exit*

JESSICA
    Farewell; and if my fortune be not crost,
    I have a father, you a daughter, lost.   *Exit*

II.6   *Enter the masquers, Gratiano and Salerio*

GRATIANO
    This is the penthouse under which Lorenzo
    Desired us to make stand.

SALERIO   His hour is almost past.

GRATIANO
    And it is marvel he outdwells his hour,
    For lovers ever run before the clock.

SALERIO
    O ten times faster Venus' pigeons fly
    To seal love's bonds new-made than they are wont

To keep obligèd faith unforfeited!

GRATIANO

That ever holds. Who riseth from a feast
With that keen appetite that he sits down?
Where is the horse that doth untread again   10
His tedious measures with the unbated fire
That he did pace them first? All things that are
Are with more spirit chasèd than enjoyed.
How like a younger or a prodigal
The scarfèd bark puts from her native bay,
Hugged and embracèd by the strumpet wind.
How like the prodigal doth she return,
With overweathered ribs and ragged sails,
Lean, rent, and beggared by the strumpet wind.
      Enter Lorenzo

SALERIO

Here comes Lorenzo; more of this hereafter.   20

LORENZO

Sweet friends, your patience for my long abode.
Not I but my affairs have made you wait.
When you shall please to play the thieves for wives,
I'll watch as long for you then. Approach.
Here dwells my father Jew. Ho! Who's within?
      Enter Jessica above, in boy's clothes

JESSICA

Who are you? Tell me for more certainty,
Albeit I'll swear that I do know your tongue.

LORENZO

Lorenzo, and thy love.

JESSICA

Lorenzo certain, and my love indeed,
For who love I so much? And now who knows   30
But you, Lorenzo, whether I am yours?

LORENZO

  Heaven and thy thoughts are witness that thou art.

JESSICA

  Here, catch this casket; it is worth the pains.

  I am glad 'tis night, you do not look on me,

  For I am much ashamed of my exchange.

  But love is blind, and lovers cannot see

  The pretty follies that themselves commit;

  For if they could, Cupid himself would blush

  To see me thus transformèd to a boy.

LORENZO

40   Descend, for you must be my torchbearer.

JESSICA

  What, must I hold a candle to my shames?

  They in themselves, good sooth, are too too light.

  Why, 'tis an office of discovery, love,

  And I should be obscured.

LORENZO   So are you, sweet,

  Even in the lovely garnish of a boy.

  But come at once,

  For the close night doth play the runaway,

  And we are stayed for at Bassanio's feast.

JESSICA

  I will make fast the doors, and gild myself

50   With some more ducats, and be with you straight.

Exit above

GRATIANO

  Now by my hood, a gentle and no Jew!

LORENZO

  Beshrew me but I love her heartily!

  For she is wise, if I can judge of her,

  And fair she is, if that mine eyes be true,

  And true she is, as she hath proved herself;

  And therefore, like herself, wise, fair, and true,

Shall she be placèd in my constant soul.

    Enter Jessica below

What, art thou come? On, gentlemen, away!

Our masquing mates by this time for us stay.

                       Exit with Jessica and Salerio

    Enter Antonio

ANTONIO

Who's there?   60

GRATIANO

Signor Antonio?

ANTONIO

Fie, fie, Gratiano! Where are all the rest?

'Tis nine o'clock; our friends all stay for you.

No masque tonight. The wind is come about;

Bassanio presently will go aboard.

I have sent twenty out to seek for you.

GRATIANO

I am glad on't. I desire no more delight

Than to be under sail and gone tonight.   *Exeunt*

    Flourish of cornets. Enter Portia with Morocco and   **II.7**
    both their trains

PORTIA

Go, draw aside the curtains and discover

The several caskets to this noble Prince.

Now make your choice.

MOROCCO

This first, of gold, who this inscription bears,

Who chooseth me shall gain what many men desire;

The second, silver, which this promise carries,

Who chooseth me shall get as much as he deserves;

This third, dull lead, with warning all as blunt,

Who chooseth me must give and hazard all he hath.

10   How shall I know if I do choose the right?

PORTIA
      The one of them contains my picture, Prince.
      If you choose that, then I am yours withal.

MOROCCO
      Some god direct my judgement! Let me see:
      I will survey th'inscriptions back again.
      What says this leaden casket?
      Who chooseth me must give and hazard all he hath.
      Must give, for what? For lead! Hazard for lead?
      This casket threatens; men that hazard all
      Do it in hope of fair advantages.
20   A golden mind stoops not to shows of dross;
      I'll then nor give nor hazard aught for lead.
      What says the silver with her virgin hue?
      Who chooseth me shall get as much as he deserves.
      As much as he deserves? Pause there, Morocco,
      And weigh thy value with an even hand.
      If thou be'st rated by thy estimation,
      Thou dost deserve enough and yet enough
      May not extend so far as to the lady,
      And yet to be afeard of my deserving
30   Were but a weak disabling of myself.
      As much as I deserve? Why that's the lady!
      I do in birth deserve her, and in fortunes,
      In graces, and in qualities of breeding;
      But more than these, in love I do deserve.
      What if I strayed no farther, but chose here?
      Let's see once more this saying graved in gold:
      Who chooseth me shall gain what many men desire.
      Why that's the lady! All the world desires her;
      From the four corners of the earth they come
40   To kiss this shrine, this mortal breathing saint.
      The Hyrcanian deserts and the vasty wilds

Of wide Arabia are as throughfares now
For princes to come view fair Portia.
The watery kingdom, whose ambitious head
Spits in the face of heaven, is no bar
To stop the foreign spirits, but they come
As o'er a brook to see fair Portia.
One of these three contains her heavenly picture.
Is't like that lead contains her? 'Twere damnation
To think so base a thought; it were too gross   50
To rib her cerecloth in the obscure grave.
Or shall I think in silver she's immured,
Being ten times undervalued to tried gold?
O sinful thought! Never so rich a gem
Was set in worse than gold. They have in England
A coin that bears the figure of an angel
Stampèd in gold – but that's insculped upon;
But here an angel in a golden bed
Lies all within. Deliver me the key.
Here do I choose, and thrive I as I may!   60

PORTIA
    There, take it, Prince, and if my form lie there,
    Then I am yours.
        He opens the golden casket

MOROCCO   O hell! What have we here?
    A carrion Death, within whose empty eye
    There is a written scroll. I'll read the writing.
        All that glisters is not gold;
        Often have you heard that told.
        Many a man his life hath sold
        But my outside to behold.
        Gilded tombs do worms infold.
        Had you been as wise as bold,   70
        Young in limbs, in judgement old,
        Your answer had not been inscrolled.

Fare you well, your suit is cold.
        Cold indeed, and labour lost.
        Then farewell heat, and welcome frost.
    Portia, adieu, I have too grieved a heart
    To take a tedious leave. Thus losers part.

                                Exit with his train. Flourish of cornets

PORTIA
    A gentle riddance. Draw the curtains, go.
    Let all of his complexion choose me so.   *Exeunt*

II.8   *Enter Salerio and Solanio*

SALERIO
    Why, man, I saw Bassanio under sail;
    With him is Gratiano gone along,
    And in their ship I am sure Lorenzo is not.

SOLANIO
    The villain Jew with outcries raised the Duke,
    Who went with him to search Bassanio's ship.

SALERIO
    He came too late, the ship was under sail,
    But there the Duke was given to understand
    That in a gondola were seen together
    Lorenzo and his amorous Jessica.
10   Besides, Antonio certified the Duke
    They were not with Bassanio in his ship.

SOLANIO
    I never heard a passion so confused,
    So strange, outrageous, and so variable
    As the dog Jew did utter in the streets:
    'My daughter! O my ducats! O my daughter!
    Fled with a Christian! O my Christian ducats!
    Justice! The law! My ducats and my daughter!
    A sealèd bag, two sealèd bags of ducats,

Of double ducats, stol'n from me by my daughter!
And jewels, two stones, two rich and precious stones,   20
Stol'n by my daughter! Justice! Find the girl!
She hath the stones upon her, and the ducats!'

SALERIO

Why, all the boys in Venice follow him,
Crying his stones, his daughter, and his ducats.

SOLANIO

Let good Antonio look he keep his day,
Or he shall pay for this.

SALERIO   Marry, well remembered.
I reasoned with a Frenchman yesterday,
Who told me, in the narrow seas that part
The French and English there miscarrièd
A vessel of our country richly fraught.   30
I thought upon Antonio when he told me,
And wished in silence that it were not his.

SOLANIO

You were best to tell Antonio what you hear,
Yet do not suddenly, for it may grieve him.

SALERIO

A kinder gentleman treads not the earth.
I saw Bassanio and Antonio part;
Bassanio told him he would make some speed
Of his return; he answered, 'Do not so.
Slubber not business for my sake, Bassanio,
But stay the very riping of the time.   40
And for the Jew's bond which he hath of me,
Let it not enter in your mind of love.
Be merry, and employ your chiefest thoughts
To courtship and such fair ostents of love
As shall conveniently become you there.'
And even there, his eye being big with tears,
Turning his face, he put his hand behind him,

And with affection wondrous sensible
He wrung Bassanio's hand; and so they parted.

SOLANIO

I think he only loves the world for him.
I pray thee let us go and find him out,
And quicken his embracèd heaviness
With some delight or other.

SALERIO   Do we so.   *Exeunt*

II.9   *Enter Nerissa and a servitor*

NERISSA

Quick, quick I pray thee! Draw the curtain straight.
The Prince of Arragon hath ta'en his oath,
And comes to his election presently.

  Flourish of cornets. Enter Arragon, his train, and Portia

PORTIA

Behold, there stand the caskets, noble Prince.
If you choose that wherein I am contained,
Straight shall our nuptial rites be solemnized;
But if you fail, without more speech, my lord,
You must be gone from hence immediately.

ARRAGON

I am enjoined by oath to observe three things:
First, never to unfold to anyone
Which casket 'twas I chose; next, if I fail
Of the right casket, never in my life
To woo a maid in way of marriage;
Lastly,
If I do fail in fortune of my choice,
Immediately to leave you and be gone.

PORTIA

To these injunctions everyone doth swear
That comes to hazard for my worthless self.

ARRAGON

And so have I addressed me. Fortune now
To my heart's hope! Gold, silver, and base lead.   20
Who chooseth me must give and hazard all he hath.
You shall look fairer ere I give or hazard.
What says the golden chest? Ha, let me see.
Who chooseth me shall gain what many men desire.
What many men desire; that 'many' may be meant
By the fool multitude that choose by show,
Not learning more than the fond eye doth teach,
Which pries not to th'interior, but like the martlet
Builds in the weather on the outward wall,
Even in the force and road of casualty.   30
I will not choose what many men desire,
Because I will not jump with common spirits
And rank me with the barbarous multitudes.
Why then, to thee, thou silver treasure house.
Tell me once more what title thou dost bear.
Who chooseth me shall get as much as he deserves.
And well said too, for who shall go about
To cozen fortune, and be honourable
Without the stamp of merit? Let none presume
To wear an undeservèd dignity.   40
O that estates, degrees, and offices
Were not derived corruptly, and that clear honour
Were purchased by the merit of the wearer!
How many then should cover that stand bare,
How many be commanded that command;
How much low peasantry would then be gleaned
From the true seed of honour, and how much honour
Picked from the chaff and ruin of the times
To be new varnished. Well, but to my choice.
Who chooseth me shall get as much as he deserves.   50
I will assume desert. Give me a key for this,

And instantly unlock my fortunes here.
He opens the silver casket

PORTIA

Too long a pause for that which you find there.

ARRAGON

What's here? The portrait of a blinking idiot
Presenting me a schedule! I will read it.
How much unlike art thou to Portia!
How much unlike my hopes and my deservings!
Who chooseth me shall have as much as he deserves.
Did I deserve no more than a fool's head?
60   Is that my prize? Are my deserts no better?

PORTIA

To offend and judge are distinct offices,
And of opposèd natures.

ARRAGON   What is here?
    The fire seven times trièd this;
    Seven times tried that judgement is
    That did never choose amiss.
    Some there be that shadows kiss;
    Such have but a shadow's bliss.
    There be fools alive iwis,
    Silvered o'er, and so was this.
70   *Take what wife you will to bed,*
    I will ever be your head.
    So be gone; you are sped.
    Still more fool I shall appear
    By the time I linger here.
    With one fool's head I came to woo,
    But I go away with two.
    Sweet, adieu. I'll keep my oath,
    Patiently to bear my wroth.   *Exit with his train*

PORTIA

Thus hath the candle singed the moth.

O these deliberate fools! When they do choose,   80
They have the wisdom by their wit to lose.

NERISSA

The ancient saying is no heresy:
Hanging and wiving goes by destiny.

PORTIA

Come draw the curtain, Nerissa.

Enter Messenger

MESSENGER

Where is my lady?

PORTIA   Here. What would my lord?

MESSENGER

Madam, there is alighted at your gate
A young Venetian, one that comes before
To signify th'approaching of his lord,
From whom he bringeth sensible regreets,
To wit, besides commends and courteous breath,   90
Gifts of rich value. Yet I have not seen
So likely an ambassador of love.
A day in April never came so sweet
To show how costly summer was at hand,
As this fore-spurrer comes before his lord.

PORTIA

No more, I pray thee, I am half afeard
Thou wilt say anon he is some kin to thee,
Thou spend'st such high-day wit in praising him.
Come, come, Nerissa, for I long to see
Quick Cupid's post that comes so mannerly.   100

NERISSA

Bassanio Lord, love if thy will it be!   *Exeunt*

*

III.I   *Enter Solanio and Salerio*

SOLANIO Now what news on the Rialto?

SALERIO Why, yet it lives there unchecked that Antonio hath a ship of rich lading wracked on the narrow seas, the Goodwins I think they call the place, a very dangerous flat, and fatal, where the carcasses of many a tall ship lie buried as they say, if my gossip Report be an honest woman of her word.

SOLANIO I would she were as lying a gossip in that as ever knapped ginger or made her neighbours believe she wept for the death of a third husband. But it is true, without any slips of prolixity or crossing the plain highway of talk, that the good Antonio, the honest Antonio — O that I had a title good enough to keep his name company . . .

SALERIO Come, the full stop!

SOLANIO Ha, what sayest thou? Why the end is, he hath lost a ship.

SALERIO I would it might prove the end of his losses.

SOLANIO Let me say amen betimes lest the devil cross my prayer, for here he comes in the likeness of a Jew.

    Enter Shylock

How now, Shylock? What news among the merchants?

SHYLOCK You knew, none so well, none so well as you, of my daughter's flight.

SALERIO That's certain. I for my part knew the tailor that made the wings she flew withal.

SOLANIO And Shylock for his own part knew the bird was fledged, and then it is the complexion of them all to leave the dam.

SHYLOCK She is damned for it.

SALERIO That's certain, if the devil may be her judge.

SHYLOCK My own flesh and blood to rebel!

SOLANIO Out upon it, old carrion! Rebels it at these years?

SHYLOCK I say my daughter is my flesh and my blood.

SALERIO There is more difference between thy flesh and
hers than between jet and ivory, more between your
bloods than there is between red wine and Rhenish. But
tell us, do you hear whether Antonio have had any loss
at sea or no?

SHYLOCK There I have another bad match! A bankrupt,   40
a prodigal, who dare scarce show his head on the Rialto,
a beggar that was used to come so smug upon the mart!
Let him look to his bond. He was wont to call me usurer.
Let him look to his bond. He was wont to lend money
for a Christian courtesy. Let him look to his bond.

SALERIO Why, I am sure if he forfeit thou wilt not take his
flesh. What's that good for?

SHYLOCK To bait fish withal. If it will feed nothing else,
it will feed my revenge. He hath disgraced me and hin-
dered me half a million, laughed at my losses, mocked at   50
my gains, scorned my nation, thwarted my bargains,
cooled my friends, heated mine enemies, and what's his
reason? I am a Jew. Hath not a Jew eyes? Hath not a
Jew hands, organs, dimensions, senses, affections, passions? Fed with the same food, hurt with the same
weapons, subject to the same diseases, healed by the
same means, warmed and cooled by the same winter and
summer as a Christian is? If you prick us, do we not
bleed? If you tickle us, do we not laugh? If you poison
us, do we not die? And if you wrong us, shall we not   60
revenge? If we are like you in the rest, we will resemble
you in that. If a Jew wrong a Christian, what is his
humility? Revenge. If a Christian wrong a Jew, what
should his sufferance be by Christian example? Why,
revenge! The villainy you teach me I will execute, and it
shall go hard but I will better the instruction.

   Enter a Man from Antonio

MAN Gentlemen, my master Antonio is at his house and
    desires to speak with you both.

SALERIO We have been up and down to seek him.

    Enter Tubal

70 SOLANIO Here comes another of the tribe. A third cannot
    be matched, unless the devil himself turn Jew.

                    Exeunt Solanio, Salerio, and Man

SHYLOCK How now, Tubal! What news from Genoa?
    Hast thou found my daughter?

TUBAL I often came where I did hear of her, but cannot
    find her.

SHYLOCK Why there, there, there, there! A diamond gone
    cost me two thousand ducats in Frankfurt! The curse
    never fell upon our nation till now; I never felt it till
    now. Two thousand ducats in that, and other precious,
80 precious jewels. I would my daughter were dead at my
    foot, and the jewels in her ear! Would she were hearsed
    at my foot, and the ducats in her coffin! No news of
    them, why so? – And I know not what's spent in the
    search. Why thou loss upon loss! The thief gone with so
    much, and so much to find the thief! – And no satisfac-
    tion, no revenge! Nor no ill luck stirring but what lights
    o'my shoulders, no sighs but o'my breathing, no tears
    but o'my shedding.

TUBAL Yes, other men have ill luck too. Antonio, as I
90 heard in Genoa . . .

SHYLOCK What, what, what? Ill luck, ill luck?

TUBAL Hath an argosy cast away coming from Tripolis.

SHYLOCK I thank God, I thank God! Is it true? Is it true?

TUBAL I spoke with some of the sailors that escaped the
    wrack.

SHYLOCK I thank thee, good Tubal. Good news, good
    news! Ha, ha! Heard in Genoa?

TUBAL Your daughter spent in Genoa, as I heard, one night
    fourscore ducats.

SHYLOCK Thou stick'st a dagger in me. I shall never see   100
my gold again. Fourscore ducats at a sitting, fourscore
ducats!

TUBAL There came divers of Antonio's creditors in my
company to Venice that swear he cannot choose but
break.

SHYLOCK I am very glad of it. I'll plague him; I'll torture
him. I am glad of it.

TUBAL One of them showed me a ring that he had of your
daughter for a monkey.

SHYLOCK Out upon her! Thou torturest me, Tubal. It   110
was my turquoise; I had it of Leah when I was a
bachelor. I would not have given it for a wilderness of
monkeys.

TUBAL But Antonio is certainly undone.

SHYLOCK Nay, that's true, that's very true. Go, Tubal,
fee me an officer; bespeak him a fortnight before. I will
have the heart of him if he forfeit, for were he out of
Venice I can make what merchandise I will. Go, Tubal,
and meet me at our synagogue; go, good Tubal; at our
synagogue, Tubal.   *Exeunt*   120

Enter Bassanio, Portia, Gratiano, Nerissa, and all   **III.2**
their trains

PORTIA
I pray you tarry, pause a day or two
Before you hazard, for in choosing wrong
I lose your company. Therefore forbear awhile.
There's something tells me, but it is not love,
I would not lose you; and you know yourself
Hate counsels not in such a quality.
But lest you should not understand me well –
And yet a maiden hath no tongue but thought –

I would detain you here some month or two
10   Before you venture for me. I could teach you
How to choose right, but then I am forsworn.
So will I never be. So may you miss me.
But if you do, you'll make me wish a sin,
That I had been forsworn. Beshrew your eyes!
They have o'erlooked me and divided me;
One half of me is yours, the other half yours,
Mine own I would say; but if mine then yours,
And so all yours. O these naughty times
Puts bars between the owners and their rights.
20   And so, though yours, not yours. Prove it so,
Let fortune go to hell for it, not I.
I speak too long, but 'tis to piece the time,
To eke it and to draw it out in length,
To stay you from election.

BASSANIO   Let me choose,
For as I am, I live upon the rack.

PORTIA
Upon the rack, Bassanio? Then confess
What treason there is mingled with your love.

BASSANIO
None but that ugly treason of mistrust
Which makes me fear th'enjoying of my love.
30   There may as well be amity and life
'Tween snow and fire, as treason and my love.

PORTIA
Ay, but I fear you speak upon the rack,
Where men enforcèd do speak anything.

BASSANIO
Promise me life and I'll confess the truth.

PORTIA
Well then, confess and live.

BASSANIO   Confess and love

Had been the very sum of my confession.
O happy torment, when my torturer
Doth teach me answers for deliverance.
But let me to my fortune and the caskets.

PORTIA

Away then, I am locked in one of them;   40
If you do love me, you will find me out.
Nerissa and the rest, stand all aloof.
Let music sound while he doth make his choice,
Then if he lose he makes a swanlike end,
Fading in music. That the comparison
May stand more proper, my eye shall be the stream
And watery deathbed for him. He may win,
And what is music then? Then music is
Even as the flourish when true subjects bow
To a new-crownèd monarch. Such it is   50
As are those dulcet sounds in break of day
That creep into the dreaming bridegroom's ear
And summon him to marriage. Now he goes,
With no less presence but with much more love
Than young Alcides when he did redeem
The virgin tribute paid by howling Troy
To the sea monster. I stand for sacrifice;
The rest aloof are the Dardanian wives,
With blearèd visages come forth to view
The issue of th'exploit. Go, Hercules;   60
Live thou, I live. With much, much more dismay
I view the fight than thou that mak'st the fray.

> *A song the whilst Bassanio comments on the caskets*
> *to himself*

>> Tell me where is fancy bred,
>> Or in the heart, or in the head?
>> How begot, how nourishèd?
>>   Reply, reply.

It is engendered in the eyes,
With gazing fed, and fancy dies
In the cradle where it lies.
70   Let us all ring fancy's knell.
      I'll begin it – Ding, dong, bell.

ALL   Ding, dong, bell.

BASSANIO

So may the outward shows be least themselves.
The world is still deceived with ornament.
In law, what plea so tainted and corrupt,
But being seasoned with a gracious voice,
Obscures the show of evil? In religion,
What damnèd error but some sober brow
Will bless it and approve it with a text,
80   Hiding the grossness with fair ornament?
There is no vice so simple but assumes
Some mark of virtue on his outward parts.
How many cowards whose hearts are all as false
As stairs of sand, wear yet upon their chins
The beards of Hercules and frowning Mars,
Who inward searched, have livers white as milk,
And these assume but valour's excrement
To render them redoubted. Look on beauty,
And you shall see 'tis purchased by the weight,
90   Which therein works a miracle in nature,
Making them lightest that wear most of it.
So are those crispèd snaky golden locks,
Which make such wanton gambols with the wind
Upon supposèd fairness, often known
To be the dowry of a second head,
The skull that bred them in the sepulchre.
Thus ornament is but the guilèd shore
To a most dangerous sea, the beauteous scarf
Veiling an Indian beauty; in a word,

The seeming truth which cunning times put on   100
To entrap the wisest. Therefore thou gaudy gold,
Hard food for Midas, I will none of thee;
Nor none of thee, thou pale and common drudge
'Tween man and man. But thou, thou meagre lead
Which rather threaten'st than dost promise aught,
Thy paleness moves me more than eloquence,
And here choose I. Joy be the consequence!

PORTIA (*aside*)

How all the other passions fleet to air:
As doubtful thoughts, and rash-embraced despair,
And shudd'ring fear, and green-eyed jealousy.   110
O love, be moderate, allay thy ecstasy,
In measure rain thy joy, scant this excess,
I feel too much thy blessing, make it less
For fear I surfeit.

BASSANIO (*opening the leaden casket*)
                          What find I here?
Fair Portia's counterfeit! What demigod
Hath come so near creation? Move these eyes?
Or whether, riding on the balls of mine,
Seem they in motion? Here are severed lips
Parted with sugar breath; so sweet a bar
Should sunder such sweet friends. Here in her hairs   120
The painter plays the spider, and hath woven
A golden mesh t'entrap the hearts of men
Faster than gnats in cobwebs. But her eyes,
How could he see to do them? Having made one,
Methinks it should have power to steal both his
And leave itself unfurnished. Yet look how far
The substance of my praise doth wrong this shadow
In underprizing it, so far this shadow
Doth limp behind the substance. Here's the scroll,
The continent and summary of my fortune: 130

You that choose not by the view
Chance as fair, and choose as true.
Since this fortune falls to you,
Be content and seek no new.
If you be well pleased with this
And hold your fortune for your bliss,
Turn you where your lady is,
And claim her with a loving kiss.

A gentle scroll. Fair lady, by your leave.
140   I come by note, to give and to receive.
Like one of two contending in a prize,
That thinks he hath done well in people's eyes,
Hearing applause and universal shout,
Giddy in spirit, still gazing in a doubt
Whether those peals of praise be his or no,
So, thrice-fair lady, stand I even so,
As doubtful whether what I see be true,
Until confirmed, signed, ratified by you.

PORTIA
You see me, Lord Bassanio, where I stand,
150   Such as I am. Though for myself alone
I would not be ambitious in my wish
To wish myself much better, yet for you
I would be trebled twenty times myself,
A thousand times more fair, ten thousand times
More rich, that only to stand high in your account,
I might in virtues, beauties, livings, friends,
Exceed account; but the full sum of me
Is sum of something, which to term in gross,
Is an unlessoned girl, unschooled, unpractisèd,
160   Happy in this, she is not yet so old
But she may learn; happier than this,
She is not bred so dull but she can learn;
Happiest of all is that her gentle spirit

Commits itself to yours to be directed,
As from her lord, her governor, her king.
Myself and what is mine to you and yours
Is now converted. But now I was the lord
Of this fair mansion, master of my servants,
Queen o'er myself; and even now, but now,
This house, these servants, and this same myself   170
Are yours, my lord's. I give them with this ring,
Which when you part from, lose, or give away,
Let it presage the ruin of your love
And be my vantage to exclaim on you.

BASSANIO

Madam, you have bereft me of all words.
Only my blood speaks to you in my veins,
And there is such confusion in my powers
As, after some oration fairly spoke
By a belovèd prince, there doth appear
Among the buzzing pleasèd multitude,   180
Where every something being blent together
Turns to a wild of nothing, save of joy
Expressed and not expressed. But when this ring
Parts from this finger, then parts life from hence,
O then be bold to say Bassanio's dead.

NERISSA

My lord and lady, it is now our time,
That have stood by and seen our wishes prosper,
To cry good joy, good joy, my lord and lady!

GRATIANO

My Lord Bassanio, and my gentle lady,
I wish you all the joy that you can wish,   190
For I am sure you can wish none from me;
And when your honours mean to solemnize
The bargain of your faith, I do beseech you
Even at that time I may be married too.

BASSANIO
With all my heart, so thou canst get a wife.

GRATIANO
I thank your lordship, you have got me one.
My eyes, my lord, can look as swift as yours:
You saw the mistress, I beheld the maid.
You loved, I loved; for intermission
200 No more pertains to me, my lord, than you.
Your fortune stood upon the caskets there,
And so did mine too, as the matter falls;
For wooing here until I sweat again,
And swearing till my very roof was dry
With oaths of love, at last, if promise last,
I got a promise of this fair one here
To have her love, provided that your fortune
Achieved her mistress.

PORTIA   Is this true, Nerissa?

NERISSA
Madam, it is, so you stand pleased withal.

BASSANIO
210 And do you, Gratiano, mean good faith?

GRATIANO
Yes, faith, my lord.

BASSANIO
Our feast shall be much honoured in your marriage.

GRATIANO We'll play with them, the first boy for a thousand ducats.

NERISSA What, and stake down?

GRATIANO No, we shall ne'er win at that sport, and stake
down.
But who comes here? Lorenzo and his infidel!
What, and my old Venetian friend Salerio!

*Enter Lorenzo, Jessica, and Salerio, a messenger
from Venice*

BASSANIO

    Lorenzo and Salerio, welcome hither,   220

    If that the youth of my new interest here

    Have power to bid you welcome. By your leave,

    I bid my very friends and countrymen,

    Sweet Portia, welcome.

PORTIA   So do I, my lord.

    They are entirely welcome.

LORENZO

    I thank your honour. For my part, my lord,

    My purpose was not to have seen you here,

    But meeting with Salerio by the way,

    He did entreat me past all saying nay

    To come with him along.

SALERIO   I did, my lord,   230

    And I have reason for it. Signor Antonio

    Commends him to you.

      He gives Bassanio a letter

BASSANIO   Ere I ope his letter,

    I pray you tell me how my good friend doth.

SALERIO

    Not sick, my lord, unless it be in mind,

    Nor well unless in mind. His letter there

    Will show you his estate.

      Bassanio opens the letter

GRATIANO

    Nerissa, cheer yond stranger; bid her welcome.

    Your hand, Salerio. What's the news from Venice?

    How doth that royal merchant, good Antonio?

    I know he will be glad of our success;   240

    We are the Jasons, we have won the Fleece.

SALERIO

    I would you had won the fleece that he hath lost.

PORTIA

There are some shrewd contents in yond same paper
That steals the colour from Bassanio's cheek:
Some dear friend dead, else nothing in the world
Could turn so much the constitution
Of any constant man. What, worse and worse?
With leave, Bassanio, I am half yourself,
And I must freely have the half of anything
250   That this same paper brings you.

BASSANIO   O sweet Portia,
Here are a few of the unpleasant'st words
That ever blotted paper! Gentle lady,
When I did first impart my love to you,
I freely told you all the wealth I had
Ran in my veins – I was a gentleman –
And then I told you true; and yet, dear lady,
Rating myself at nothing, you shall see
How much I was a braggart. When I told you
My state was nothing, I should then have told you
260   That I was worse than nothing; for indeed
I have engaged myself to a dear friend,
Engaged my friend to his mere enemy
To feed my means. Here is a letter, lady,
The paper as the body of my friend,
And every word in it a gaping wound
Issuing life-blood. But is it true, Salerio?
Hath all his ventures failed? What, not one hit?
From Tripolis, from Mexico and England,
From Lisbon, Barbary, and India,
270   And not one vessel scape the dreadful touch
Of merchant-marring rocks?

SALERIO   Not one, my lord.
Besides, it should appear that if he had
The present money to discharge the Jew,

He would not take it. Never did I know
A creature that did bear the shape of man
So keen and greedy to confound a man.
He plies the Duke at morning and at night,
And doth impeach the freedom of the state
If they deny him justice. Twenty merchants,
The Duke himself, and the magnificoes   280
Of greatest port have all persuaded with him,
But none can drive him from the envious plea
Of forfeiture, of justice, and his bond.

JESSICA

When I was with him, I have heard him swear
To Tubal and to Chus, his countrymen,
That he would rather have Antonio's flesh
Than twenty times the value of the sum
That he did owe him, and I know, my lord,
If law, authority, and power deny not,
It will go hard with poor Antonio.   290

PORTIA

Is it your dear friend that is thus in trouble?

BASSANIO

The dearest friend to me, the kindest man,
The best-conditioned and unwearied spirit
In doing courtesies, and one in whom
The ancient Roman honour more appears
Than any that draws breath in Italy.

PORTIA

What sum owes he the Jew?

BASSANIO

For me, three thousand ducats.

PORTIA   What, no more?
Pay him six thousand, and deface the bond.
Double six thousand and then treble that,   300
Before a friend of this description

Shall lose a hair through Bassanio's fault.
First go with me to church and call me wife,
And then away to Venice to your friend!
For never shall you lie by Portia's side
With an unquiet soul. You shall have gold
To pay the petty debt twenty times over.
When it is paid, bring your true friend along.
My maid Nerissa and myself meantime
310 Will live as maids and widows. Come away,
For you shall hence upon your wedding day.
Bid your friends welcome, show a merry cheer;
Since you are dear bought, I will love you dear.
But let me hear the letter of your friend.

BASSANIO *Sweet Bassanio, my ships have all miscarried,
my creditors grow cruel, my estate is very low, my bond
to the Jew is forfeit. And since in paying it, it is impossible
I should live, all debts are cleared between you and I if I
might but see you at my death. Notwithstanding, use your*
320 *pleasure. If your love do not persuade you to come, let not
my letter.*

PORTIA
O love, dispatch all business and be gone.

BASSANIO
Since I have your good leave to go away,
I will make haste, but till I come again
No bed shall e'er be guilty of my stay,
Nor rest be interposer 'twixt us twain.   *Exeunt*

III.3   *Enter Shylock the Jew and Solanio and Antonio and
the gaoler*

SHYLOCK
Gaoler, look to him. Tell not me of mercy.
This is the fool that lent out money gratis.

Gaoler, look to him.

ANTONIO   Hear me yet, good Shylock.

SHYLOCK
I'll have my bond! Speak not against my bond!
I have sworn an oath that I will have my bond.
Thou call'dst me dog before thou hadst a cause,
But since I am a dog, beware my fangs.
The Duke shall grant me justice. I do wonder,
Thou naughty gaoler, that thou art so fond
To come abroad with him at his request.   10

ANTONIO
I pray thee hear me speak.

SHYLOCK
I'll have my bond. I will not hear thee speak.
I'll have my bond, and therefore speak no more.
I'll not be made a soft and dull-eyed fool,
To shake the head, relent, and sigh, and yield
To Christian intercessors. Follow not.
I'll have no speaking, I will have my bond.   *Exit*

SOLANIO
It is the most impenetrable cur
That ever kept with men.

ANTONIO   Let him alone.
I'll follow him no more with bootless prayers.   20
He seeks my life. His reason well I know:
I oft delivered from his forfeitures
Many that have at times made moan to me.
Therefore he hates me.

SOLANIO   I am sure the Duke
Will never grant this forfeiture to hold.

ANTONIO
The Duke cannot deny the course of law,
For the commodity that strangers have
With us in Venice, if it be denied,

Will much impeach the justice of the state,
30 Since that the trade and profit of the city
Consisteth of all nations. Therefore go.
These griefs and losses have so bated me
That I shall hardly spare a pound of flesh
Tomorrow to my bloody creditor.
Well, Gaoler, on. Pray Bassanio come
To see me pay his debt, and then I care not.   *Exeunt*

III.4   *Enter Portia, Nerissa, Lorenzo, Jessica, and*
                 Balthasar, a man of Portia's

LORENZO
Madam, although I speak it in your presence,
You have a noble and a true conceit
Of godlike amity, which appears most strongly
In bearing thus the absence of your lord.
But if you knew to whom you show this honour,
How true a gentleman you send relief,
How dear a lover of my lord your husband,
I know you would be prouder of the work
Than customary bounty can enforce you.

PORTIA
10 I never did repent for doing good,
Nor shall not now; for in companions
That do converse and waste the time together,
Whose souls do bear an equal yoke of love,
There must be needs a like proportion
Of lineaments, of manners, and of spirit;
Which makes me think that this Antonio,
Being the bosom lover of my lord,
Must needs be like my lord. If it be so,
How little is the cost I have bestowed
20 In purchasing the semblance of my soul

From out the state of hellish cruelty.
This comes too near the praising of myself,
Therefore no more of it. Hear other things:
Lorenzo, I commit into your hands
The husbandry and manage of my house
Until my lord's return. For mine own part,
I have toward heaven breathed a secret vow
To live in prayer and contemplation,
Only attended by Nerissa here,
Until her husband and my lord's return.   30
There is a monastery two miles off,
And there we will abide. I do desire you
Not to deny this imposition,
The which my love and some necessity
Now lays upon you.

LORENZO   Madam, with all my heart,
I shall obey you in all fair commands.

PORTIA
My people do already know my mind
And will acknowledge you and Jessica
In place of Lord Bassanio and myself.
So fare you well till we shall meet again.   40

LORENZO
Fair thoughts and happy hours attend on you!

JESSICA
I wish your ladyship all heart's content.

PORTIA
I thank you for your wish, and am well pleased
To wish it back on you. Fare you well, Jessica.

                    Exeunt Jessica and Lorenzo
Now, Balthasar,
As I have ever found thee honest-true,
So let me find thee still. Take this same letter,
And use thou all th'endeavour of a man

In speed to Padua. See thou render this
50 Into my cousin's hand, Doctor Bellario,
And look what notes and garments he doth give thee
Bring them, I pray thee, with imagined speed
Unto the traject, to the common ferry
Which trades to Venice. Waste no time in words
But get thee gone. I shall be there before thee.

BALTHASAR
Madam, I go with all convenient speed.   *Exit*

PORTIA
Come on, Nerissa; I have work in hand
That you yet know not of. We'll see our husbands
Before they think of us.

NERISSA   Shall they see us?

PORTIA
60 They shall, Nerissa, but in such a habit
That they shall think we are accomplishèd
With that we lack. I'll hold thee any wager,
When we are both accoutered like young men,
I'll prove the prettier fellow of the two,
And wear my dagger with the braver grace,
And speak between the change of man and boy
With a reed voice, and turn two mincing steps
Into a manly stride, and speak of frays
Like a fine bragging youth, and tell quaint lies,
70 How honourable ladies sought my love,
Which I denying, they fell sick and died –
I could not do withal. Then I'll repent,
And wish, for all that, that I had not killed them.
And twenty of these puny lies I'll tell,
That men shall swear I have discontinued school
Above a twelve month. I have within my mind
A thousand raw tricks of these bragging Jacks,
Which I will practise.

NERISSA   Why, shall we turn to men?

PORTIA

Fie, what a question's that,
If thou wert near a lewd interpreter!   80
But come, I'll tell thee all my whole device
When I am in my coach, which stays for us
At the park gate, and therefore haste away,
For we must measure twenty miles today.   *Exeunt*

Enter Launcelot the Clown and Jessica   III.5

LAUNCELOT Yes truly, for look you, the sins of the father
    are to be laid upon the children. Therefore, I promise
    you I fear you. I was always plain with you, and so now
    I speak my agitation of the matter. Therefore be o'good
    cheer, for truly I think you are damned. There is but
    one hope in it that can do you any good, and that is but a
    kind of bastard hope neither.

JESSICA And what hope is that, I pray thee?

LAUNCELOT Marry, you may partly hope that your father
    got you not, that you are not the Jew's daughter.   10

JESSICA That were a kind of bastard hope indeed! So the
    sins of my mother should be visited upon me.

LAUNCELOT Truly then, I fear you are damned both by
    father and mother. Thus when I shun Scylla your father,
    I fall into Charybdis your mother. Well, you are gone
    both ways.

JESSICA I shall be saved by my husband. He hath made
    me a Christian.

LAUNCELOT Truly, the more to blame he! We were
    Christians enow before, e'en as many as could well live   20
    one by another. This making of Christians will raise the
    price of hogs; if we grow all to be pork-eaters, we shall
    not shortly have a rasher on the coals for money.

Enter Lorenzo

JESSICA I'll tell my husband, Launcelot, what you say.
Here he comes.

LORENZO I shall grow jealous of you shortly, Launcelot,
if you thus get my wife into corners.

JESSICA Nay, you need not fear us, Lorenzo. Launcelot
and I are out. He tells me flatly there's no mercy for me
30   in heaven because I am a Jew's daughter, and he says you
are no good member of the commonwealth, for in converting Jews to Christians you raise the price of pork.

LORENZO (*to Launcelot*) I shall answer that better to the
commonwealth than you can the getting up of the
Negro's belly. The Moor is with child by you, Launcelot.

LAUNCELOT It is much that the Moor should be more
than reason; but if she be less than an honest woman,
she is indeed more than I took her for.

40   LORENZO How every fool can play upon the word! I think
the best grace of wit will shortly turn into silence, and
discourse grow commendable in none only but parrots.
Go in, sirrah, bid them prepare for dinner.

LAUNCELOT That is done, sir. They have all stomachs.

LORENZO Goodly Lord, what a wit-snapper are you!
Then bid them prepare dinner.

LAUNCELOT That is done too, sir. Only 'cover' is the
word.

LORENZO Will you cover then, sir?

50   LAUNCELOT Not so, sir, neither. I know my duty.

LORENZO Yet more quarrelling with occasion. Wilt thou
show the whole wealth of thy wit in an instant? I pray
thee understand a plain man in his plain meaning: go
to thy fellows, bid them cover the table, serve in the
meat, and we will come in to dinner.

LAUNCELOT For the table, sir, it shall be served in; for

the meat, sir, it shall be covered; for your coming in to
dinner, sir, why let it be as humours and conceits shall
govern.   *Exit Launcelot*

LORENZO
O dear discretion, how his words are suited!   60
The fool hath planted in his memory
An army of good words; and I do know
A many fools that stand in better place,
Garnished like him, that for a tricksy word
Defy the matter. How cheer'st thou, Jessica?
And now, good sweet, say thy opinion,
How dost thou like the Lord Bassanio's wife?

JESSICA
Past all expressing. It is very meet
The Lord Bassanio live an upright life,
For having such a blessing in his lady,   70
He finds the joys of heaven here on earth,
And if on earth he do not merit it,
In reason he should never come to heaven.
Why, if two gods should play some heavenly match
And on the wager lay two earthly women,
And Portia one, there must be something else
Pawned with the other, for the poor rude world
Hath not her fellow.

LORENZO   Even such a husband
Hast thou of me as she is for a wife.

JESSICA
Nay, but ask my opinion too of that!   80

LORENZO
I will anon. First let us go to dinner.

JESSICA
Nay, let me praise you while I have a stomach.

LORENZO
No, pray thee, let it serve for table-talk,

Then howsome'er thou speak'st, 'mong other things
I shall digest it.

JESSICA   Well, I'll set you forth.   *Exeunt*

*

IV.1   *Enter the Duke, the magnificoes, Antonio, Bassanio,*
            Salerio, and Gratiano with others

DUKE
What, is Antonio here?

ANTONIO
Ready, so please your grace.

DUKE
I am sorry for thee. Thou art come to answer
A stony adversary, an inhuman wretch,
Uncapable of pity, void and empty
From any dram of mercy.

ANTONIO   I have heard
Your grace hath ta'en great pains to qualify
His rigorous course; but since he stands obdurate,
And that no lawful means can carry me
10   Out of his envy's reach, I do oppose
My patience to his fury, and am armed
To suffer with a quietness of spirit
The very tyranny and rage of his.

DUKE
Go one, and call the Jew into the court.

SALERIO
He is ready at the door; he comes, my lord.
      Enter Shylock

DUKE
Make room, and let him stand before our face.
Shylock, the world thinks, and I think so too,

That thou but lead'st this fashion of thy malice
To the last hour of act, and then 'tis thought
Thou'lt show thy mercy and remorse more strange   20
Than is thy strange apparent cruelty;
And where thou now exacts the penalty,
Which is a pound of this poor merchant's flesh,
Thou wilt not only loose the forfeiture,
But touched with human gentleness and love,
Forgive a moiety of the principal,
Glancing an eye of pity on his losses,
That have of late so huddled on his back,
Enow to press a royal merchant down
And pluck commiseration of his state   30
From brassy bosoms and rough hearts of flint,
From stubborn Turks and Tartars never trained
To officers of tender courtesy.
We all expect a gentle answer, Jew.

SHYLOCK

I have possessed your grace of what I purpose,
And by our holy Sabbath have I sworn
To have the due and forfeit of my bond.
If you deny it, let the danger light
Upon your charter and your city's freedom!
You'll ask me why I rather choose to have   40
A weight of carrion flesh than to receive
Three thousand ducats. I'll not answer that,
But say it is my humour. Is it answered?
What if my house be troubled with a rat,
And I be pleased to give ten thousand ducats
To have it baned? What, are you answered yet?
Some men there are love not a gaping pig,
Some that are mad if they behold a cat,
And others, when the bagpipe sings i'th'nose,
Cannot contain their urine; for affection,   50

Master of passion, sways it to the mood
Of what it likes or loathes. Now for your answer:
As there is no firm reason to be rendered
Why he cannot abide a gaping pig,
Why he a harmless necessary cat,
Why he a woollen bagpipe, but of force
Must yield to such inevitable shame
As to offend, himself being offended;
So can I give no reason, nor I will not,
More than a lodged hate and a certain loathing
I bear Antonio, that I follow thus
A losing suit against him. Are you answered?

BASSANIO
This is no answer, thou unfeeling man,
To excuse the current of thy cruelty.

SHYLOCK
I am not bound to please thee with my answers.

BASSANIO
Do all men kill the things they do not love?

SHYLOCK
Hates any man the thing he would not kill?

BASSANIO
Every offence is not a hate at first.

SHYLOCK
What, wouldst thou have a serpent sting thee twice?

ANTONIO
I pray you think you question with the Jew.
You may as well go stand upon the beach
And bid the main flood bate his usual height,
You may as well use question with the wolf
Why he hath made the ewe bleat for the lamb,
You may as well forbid the mountain pines
To wag their high-tops and to make no noise
When they are fretten with the gusts of heaven;

You may as well do anything most hard
As seek to soften that — than which what's harder? —
His Jewish heart. Therefore I do beseech you   80
Make no more offers, use no farther means,
But with all brief and plain conveniency
Let me have judgement, and the Jew his will.

BASSANIO

For thy three thousand ducats here is six.

SHYLOCK

If every ducat in six thousand ducats
Were in six parts, and every part a ducat,
I would not draw them. I would have my bond.

DUKE

How shalt thou hope for mercy, rendering none?

SHYLOCK

What judgement shall I dread, doing no wrong?
You have among you many a purchased slave,   90
Which like your asses and your dogs and mules
You use in abject and in slavish parts,
Because you bought them. Shall I say to you,
'Let them be free! Marry them to your heirs!
Why sweat they under burdens? Let their beds
Be made as soft as yours, and let their palates
Be seasoned with such viands'? You will answer,
'The slaves are ours.' So do I answer you.
The pound of flesh which I demand of him
Is dearly bought, 'tis mine, and I will have it.   100
If you deny me, fie upon your law!
There is no force in the decrees of Venice.
I stand for judgement. Answer; shall I have it?

DUKE

Upon my power I may dismiss this court
Unless Bellario, a learned doctor
Whom I have sent for to determine this,
Come here today.

SALERIO   My lord, here stays without
A messenger with letters from the doctor,
New come from Padua.

DUKE
Bring us the letters. Call the messenger.

BASSANIO
Good cheer, Antonio! What, man, courage yet!
The Jew shall have my flesh, blood, bones, and all,
Ere thou shalt lose for me one drop of blood.

ANTONIO
I am a tainted wether of the flock,
Meetest for death. The weakest kind of fruit
Drops earliest to the ground, and so let me.
You cannot better be employed, Bassanio,
Than to live still, and write mine epitaph.

Enter Nerissa dressed like a lawyer's clerk

DUKE
Came you from Padua, from Bellario?

NERISSA
From both, my lord. Bellario greets your grace.

She presents a letter

BASSANIO
Why dost thou whet thy knife so earnestly?

SHYLOCK
To cut the forfeiture from that bankrupt there.

GRATIANO
Not on thy sole, but on thy soul, harsh Jew,
Thou mak'st thy knife keen; but no metal can,
No, not the hangman's axe, bear half the keenness
Of thy sharp envy. Can no prayers pierce thee?

SHYLOCK
No, none that thou hast wit enough to make.

GRATIANO
O be thou damned, inexecrable dog,

And for thy life let justice be accused!
Thou almost mak'st me waver in my faith,   130
To hold opinion with Pythagoras
That souls of animals infuse themselves
Into the trunks of men. Thy currish spirit
Governed a wolf who, hanged for human slaughter,
Even from the gallows did his fell soul fleet,
And whilst thou layest in thy unhallowed dam,
Infused itself in thee; for thy desires
Are wolvish, bloody, starved, and ravenous.

SHYLOCK
Till thou canst rail the seal from off my bond,
Thou but offend'st thy lungs to speak so loud.   140
Repair thy wit, good youth, or it will fall
To cureless ruin. I stand here for law.

DUKE
This letter from Bellario doth commend
A young and learned doctor to our court.
Where is he?

NERISSA   He attendeth here hard by
To know your answer whether you'll admit him.

DUKE
With all my heart. Some three or four of you
Go give him courteous conduct to this place.
Meantime the court shall hear Bellario's letter.

CLERK *Your grace shall understand that at the receipt of* 150
your letter I am very sick; but in the instant that your
messenger came, in loving visitation was with me a young
doctor of Rome. His name is Balthasar. I acquainted
him with the cause in controversy between the Jew and
Antonio the merchant. We turned o'er many books to-
gether. He is furnished with my opinion which, bettered
with his own learning, the greatness whereof I cannot
enough commend, comes with him at my importunity to fill

up your grace's request in my stead. I beseech you let his
160 *lack of years be no impediment to let him lack a reverend*
estimation, for I never knew so young a body with so old a
head. I leave him to your gracious acceptance, whose trial
shall better publish his commendation.

Enter Portia as Balthasar, dressed like a Doctor of Laws

DUKE
You hear the learn'd Bellario, what he writes,
And here, I take it, is the doctor come.
Give me your hand. Came you from old Bellario?

PORTIA
I did, my lord.

DUKE   You are welcome; take your place.
Are you acquainted with the difference
That holds this present question in the court?

PORTIA
170 I am informèd throughly of the cause.
Which is the merchant here? And which the Jew?

DUKE
Antonio and old Shylock, both stand forth.

PORTIA
Is your name Shylock?

SHYLOCK   Shylock is my name.

PORTIA
Of a strange nature is the suit you follow,
Yet in such rule that the Venetian law
Cannot impugn you as you do proceed.
(*To Antonio*) You stand within his danger, do you not?

ANTONIO
Ay, so he says.

PORTIA   Do you confess the bond?

ANTONIO
I do.

PORTIA Then must the Jew be merciful.

SHYLOCK

On what compulsion must I? Tell me that.   180

PORTIA

The quality of mercy is not strained,
It droppeth as the gentle rain from heaven
Upon the place beneath. It is twice blest,
It blesseth him that gives and him that takes.
'Tis mightiest in the mightiest, it becomes
The thronèd monarch better than his crown.
His sceptre shows the force of temporal power,
The attribute to awe and majesty,
Wherein doth sit the dread and fear of kings;
But mercy is above this sceptred sway,   190
It is enthronèd in the hearts of kings,
It is an attribute to God himself,
And earthly power doth then show likest God's
When mercy seasons justice. Therefore, Jew,
Though justice be thy plea, consider this:
That in the course of justice none of us
Should see salvation. We do pray for mercy,
And that same prayer doth teach us all to render
The deeds of mercy. I have spoke thus much
To mitigate the justice of thy plea,   200
Which if thou follow, this strict court of Venice
Must needs give sentence 'gainst the merchant there.

SHYLOCK

My deeds upon my head! I crave the law,
The penalty and forfeit of my bond.

PORTIA

Is he not able to discharge the money?

BASSANIO

Yes, here I tender it for him in the court,
Yea, twice the sum. If that will not suffice,

I will be bound to pay it ten times o'er
On forfeit of my hands, my head, my heart.
210 If this will not suffice, it must appear
That malice bears down truth. And I beseech you,
Wrest once the law to your authority,
To do a great right, do a little wrong,
And curb this cruel devil of his will.

PORTIA

It must not be. There is no power in Venice
Can alter a decree establishèd.
'Twill be recorded for a precedent,
And many an error by the same example
Will rush into the state. It cannot be.

SHYLOCK

220 A Daniel come to judgement! Yea, a Daniel!
O wise young judge, how I do honour thee!

PORTIA

I pray you let me look upon the bond.

SHYLOCK

Here 'tis, most reverend doctor, here it is.

PORTIA

Shylock, there's thrice thy money offered thee.

SHYLOCK

An oath, an oath! I have an oath in heaven;
Shall I lay perjury upon my soul?
No, not for Venice!

PORTIA   Why, this bond is forfeit,
And lawfully by this the Jew may claim
A pound of flesh, to be by him cut off
230 Nearest the merchant's heart. Be merciful,
Take thrice thy money, bid me tear the bond.

SHYLOCK

When it is paid, according to the tenour.
It doth appear you are a worthy judge,

You know the law, your exposition
Hath been most sound. I charge you by the law,
Whereof you are a well-deserving pillar,
Proceed to judgement. By my soul I swear
There is no power in the tongue of man
To alter me. I stay here on my bond.

ANTONIO

Most heartily I do beseech the court   240
To give the judgement.

PORTIA   Why then, thus it is:
You must prepare your bosom for his knife.

SHYLOCK

O noble judge! O excellent young man!

PORTIA

For the intent and purpose of the law
Hath full relation to the penalty,
Which here appeareth due upon the bond.

SHYLOCK

'Tis very true. O wise and upright judge!
How much more elder art thou than thy looks!

PORTIA

Therefore lay bare your bosom.

SHYLOCK   Ay, his breast,
So says the bond, doth it not, noble judge?   250
'Nearest his heart', those are the very words.

PORTIA

It is so. Are there balance here to weigh
The flesh?

SHYLOCK   I have them ready.

PORTIA

Have by some surgeon, Shylock, on your charge,
To stop his wounds, lest he do bleed to death.

SHYLOCK

Is it so nominated in the bond?

PORTIA

It is not so expressed, but what of that?
'Twere good you do so much for charity.

SHYLOCK

I cannot find it; 'tis not in the bond.

PORTIA

260   You, merchant, have you anything to say?

ANTONIO

But little. I am armed and well prepared.
Give me your hand, Bassanio, fare you well.
Grieve not that I am fallen to this for you,
For herein Fortune shows herself more kind
Than is her custom; it is still her use
To let the wretched man outlive his wealth
To view with hollow eye and wrinkled brow
An age of poverty, from which lingering penance
Of such misery doth she cut me off.
270   Commend me to your honourable wife,
Tell her the process of Antonio's end,
Say how I loved you, speak me fair in death,
And when the tale is told, bid her be judge
Whether Bassanio had not once a love.
Repent but you that you shall lose your friend,
And he repents not that he pays your debt,
For if the Jew do cut but deep enough,
I'll pay it instantly with all my heart.

BASSANIO

Antonio, I am married to a wife
280   Which is as dear to me as life itself,
But life itself, my wife, and all the world
Are not with me esteemed above thy life.
I would lose all, ay sacrifice them all
Here to this devil, to deliver you.

PORTIA

    Your wife would give you little thanks for that
    If she were by to hear you make the offer.

GRATIANO

    I have a wife who I protest I love;
    I would she were in heaven, so she could
    Entreat some power to change this currish Jew.

NERISSA

    'Tis well you offer it behind her back,   290
    The wish would make else an unquiet house.

SHYLOCK

    These be the Christian husbands! I have a daughter;
    Would any of the stock of Barabbas
    Had been her husband, rather than a Christian.
    We trifle time. I pray thee pursue sentence.

PORTIA

    A pound of that same merchant's flesh is thine,
    The court awards it, and the law doth give it.

SHYLOCK

    Most rightful judge!

PORTIA

    And you must cut this flesh from off his breast,
    The law allows it, and the court awards it.   300

SHYLOCK

    Most learned judge! A sentence! Come, prepare!

PORTIA

    Tarry a little, there is something else.
    This bond doth give thee here no jot of blood;
    The words expressly are 'a pound of flesh'.
    Take then thy bond, take thou thy pound of flesh,
    But in the cutting it if thou dost shed
    One drop of Christian blood, thy lands and goods
    Are by the laws of Venice confiscate
    Unto the state of Venice.

GRATIANO

310   O upright judge! Mark, Jew. O learned judge!

SHYLOCK

Is that the law?

PORTIA   Thyself shalt see the act,
For, as thou urgest justice, be assured
Thou shalt have justice more than thou desir'st.

GRATIANO

O learned judge! Mark, Jew. A learned judge!

SHYLOCK

I take this offer then. Pay the bond thrice
And let the Christian go.

BASSANIO   Here is the money.

PORTIA

Soft!
The Jew shall have all justice. Soft, no haste,
He shall have nothing but the penalty.

GRATIANO

320   O Jew! An upright judge, a learned judge!

PORTIA

Therefore prepare thee to cut off the flesh.
Shed thou no blood, nor cut thou less nor more
But just a pound of flesh. If thou tak'st more
Or less than a just pound, be it but so much
As makes it light or heavy in the substance
Or the division of the twentieth part
Of one poor scruple, nay, if the scale do turn
But in the estimation of a hair,
Thou diest, and all thy goods are confiscate.

GRATIANO

330   A second Daniel! A Daniel, Jew!
Now, infidel, I have you on the hip!

PORTIA

Why doth the Jew pause? Take thy forfeiture.

SHYLOCK
Give me my principal, and let me go.

BASSANIO
I have it ready for thee; here it is.

PORTIA
He hath refused it in the open court.
He shall have merely justice and his bond.

GRATIANO
A Daniel still say I, a second Daniel!
I thank thee, Jew, for teaching me that word.

SHYLOCK
Shall I not have barely my principal?

PORTIA
Thou shalt have nothing but the forfeiture,   340
To be so taken at thy peril, Jew.

SHYLOCK
Why, then the devil give him good of it!
I'll stay no longer question.

PORTIA   Tarry, Jew!
The law hath yet another hold on you.
It is enacted in the laws of Venice,
If it be proved against an alien
That by direct or indirect attempts
He seek the life of any citizen,
The party 'gainst the which he doth contrive
Shall seize one half his goods, the other half   350
Comes to the privy coffer of the state,
And the offender's life lies in the mercy
Of the Duke only, 'gainst all other voice,
In which predicament I say thou stand'st,
For it appears by manifest proceeding
That indirectly, and directly too,
Thou hast contrived against the very life
Of the defendant, and thou hast incurred

The danger formerly by me rehearsed.
360   Down therefore, and beg mercy of the Duke.

GRATIANO

Beg that thou mayst have leave to hang thyself,
And yet, thy wealth being forfeit to the state,
Thou hast not left the value of a cord,
Therefore thou must be hanged at the state's charge.

DUKE

That thou shalt see the difference of our spirit,
I pardon thee thy life before thou ask it.
For half thy wealth, it is Antonio's,
The other half comes to the general state,
Which humbleness may drive unto a fine.

PORTIA

370   Ay, for the state, not for Antonio.

SHYLOCK

Nay, take my life and all! Pardon not that!
You take my house when you do take the prop
That doth sustain my house. You take my life
When you do take the means whereby I live.

PORTIA

What mercy can you render him, Antonio?

GRATIANO.

A halter gratis! Nothing else, for God's sake!

ANTONIO

So please my lord the Duke and all the court
To quit the fine for one half of his goods,
I am content, so he will let me have
380   The other half in use, to render it
Upon his death unto the gentleman
That lately stole his daughter.
Two things provided more: that for this favour
He presently become a Christian;
The other, that he do record a gift

Here in the court of all he dies possessed
Unto his son Lorenzo and his daughter.

DUKE

He shall do this, or else I do recant
The pardon that I late pronouncèd here.

PORTIA

Art thou contented, Jew? What dost thou say?   390

SHYLOCK

I am content.

PORTIA   Clerk, draw a deed of gift.

SHYLOCK

I pray you give me leave to go from hence,
I am not well; send the deed after me,
And I will sign it.

DUKE   Get thee gone, but do it.

GRATIANO

In christ'ning shalt thou have two godfathers.
Had I been judge, thou shouldst have had ten more,
To bring thee to the gallows, not to the font.

Exit Shylock

DUKE

Sir, I entreat you home with me to dinner.

PORTIA

I humbly do desire your grace of pardon.
I must away this night toward Padua,   400
And it is meet I presently set forth.

DUKE

I am sorry that your leisure serves you not.
Antonio, gratify this gentleman,
For in my mind you are much bound to him.

Exit Duke and his train

BASSANIO

Most worthy gentleman, I and my friend
Have by your wisdom been this day acquitted

Of grievous penalties, in lieu whereof
Three thousand ducats due unto the Jew
We freely cope your courteous pains withal.

ANTONIO

410 And stand indebted, over and above,
In love and service to you evermore.

PORTIA

He is well paid that is well satisfied,
And I delivering you am satisfied,
And therein do account myself well paid;
My mind was never yet more mercenary.
I pray you know me when we meet again,
I wish you well, and so I take my leave.

BASSANIO

Dear sir, of force I must attempt you further.
Take some remembrance of us as a tribute,
420 Not as fee. Grant me two things, I pray you:
Not to deny me, and to pardon me.

PORTIA

You press me far, and therefore I will yield.
Give me your gloves, I'll wear them for your sake.
Bassanio takes off his gloves
And for your love I'll take this ring from you.
Do not draw back your hand, I'll take no more,
And you in love shall not deny me this.

BASSANIO

This ring, good sir, alas, it is a trifle!
I will not shame myself to give you this.

PORTIA

I will have nothing else but only this,
430 And now methinks I have a mind to it.

BASSANIO

There's more depends on this than on the value.
The dearest ring in Venice will I give you,

And find it out by proclamation.
Only for this, I pray you pardon me.

PORTIA

I see, sir, you are liberal in offers.
You taught me first to beg, and now methinks
You teach me how a beggar should be answered.

BASSANIO

Good sir, this ring was given me by my wife,
And when she put it on she made me vow
That I should neither sell nor give nor lose it.   440

PORTIA

That 'scuse serves many men to save their gifts,
And if your wife be not a madwoman,
And know how well I have deserved this ring,
She would not hold out enemy for ever
For giving it to me. Well, peace be with you!

                              Exeunt Portia and Nerissa

ANTONIO

My Lord Bassanio, let him have the ring.
Let his deservings, and my love withal,
Be valued 'gainst your wife's commandèment.

BASSANIO

Go, Gratiano, run and overtake him,
Give him the ring and bring him if thou canst   450
Unto Antonio's house. Away, make haste!

                                        Exit Gratiano

Come, you and I will thither presently,
And in the morning early will we both
Fly toward Belmont. Come, Antonio.   *Exeunt*

Enter Portia and Nerissa, disguised as before   **IV.2**

PORTIA

Inquire the Jew's house out, give him this deed,

And let him sign it. We'll away tonight
And be a day before our husbands home.
This deed will be well welcome to Lorenzo.

Enter Gratiano

GRATIANO
Fair sir, you are well o'erta'en.
My Lord Bassanio upon more advice
Hath sent you here this ring, and doth entreat
Your company at dinner.

PORTIA   That cannot be.
His ring I do accept most thankfully,
And so I pray you tell him. Furthermore,
I pray you show my youth old Shylock's house.

GRATIANO
That will I do.

NERISSA   Sir, I would speak with you.
(*Aside to Portia*) I'll see if I can get my husband's ring,
Which I did make him swear to keep for ever.

PORTIA (*aside to Nerissa*)
Thou mayst, I warrant. We shall have old swearing
That they did give the rings away to men,
But we'll outface them, and outswear them too.
Away, make haste. Thou know'st where I will tarry.

NERISSA
Come, good sir, will you show me to this house?

                                        Exeunt

*

V. I   *Enter Lorenzo and Jessica*

LORENZO
The moon shines bright. In such a night as this,
When the sweet wind did gently kiss the trees

And they did make no noise, in such a night
Troilus methinks mounted the Troyan walls,
And sighed his soul toward the Grecian tents
Where Cressid lay that night.

JESSICA   In such a night
Did Thisbe fearfully o'ertrip the dew,
And saw the lion's shadow ere himself,
And ran dismayed away.

LORENZO   In such a night
Stood Dido with a willow in her hand   10
Upon the wild sea banks, and waft her love
To come again to Carthage.

JESSICA   In such a night
Medea gathered the enchanted herbs
That did renew old Aeson.

LORENZO   In such a night
Did Jessica steal from the wealthy Jew,
And with an unthrift love did run from Venice
As far as Belmont.

JESSICA   In such a night
Did young Lorenzo swear he loved her well,
Stealing her soul with many vows of faith,
And ne'er a true one.

LORENZO   In such a night   20
Did pretty Jessica, like a little shrew,
Slander her love, and he forgave it her.

JESSICA
I would out-night you, did nobody come;
But hark, I hear the footing of a man.
    Enter Stephano

LORENZO
Who comes so fast in silence of the night?

STEPHANO
A friend.

LORENZO
    A friend? What friend? Your name I pray you, friend.
STEPHANO
    Stephano is my name, and I bring word
    My mistress will before the break of day
30 Be here at Belmont. She doth stray about
    By holy crosses where she kneels and prays
    For happy wedlock hours.
LORENZO   Who comes with her?
STEPHANO
    None but a holy hermit and her maid.
    I pray you, is my master yet returned?
LORENZO
    He is not, nor we have not heard from him.
    But go we in, I pray thee, Jessica,
    And ceremoniously let us prepare
    Some welcome for the mistress of the house.
        Enter Launcelot
LAUNCELOT Sola, sola! Wo ha ho! Sola, sola!
40 LORENZO Who calls?
LAUNCELOT Sola! Did you see Master Lorenzo? Master
    Lorenzo! Sola, sola!
LORENZO Leave holloaing, man! Here.
LAUNCELOT Sola! Where? Where?
LORENZO Here!
LAUNCELOT Tell him there's a post come from my
    master, with his horn full of good news. My master will
    be here ere morning.   *Exit*
LORENZO
    Sweet soul, let's in, and there expect their coming.
50 And yet no matter, why should we go in?
    My friend Stephano, signify, I pray you,
    Within the house, your mistress is at hand,
    And bring your music forth into the air. *Exit Stephano*

How sweet the moonlight sleeps upon this bank!
Here will we sit and let the sounds of music
Creep in our ears; soft stillness and the night
Become the touches of sweet harmony.
Sit, Jessica. Look how the floor of heaven
Is thick inlaid with patens of bright gold.
There's not the smallest orb which thou beholdest   60
But in his motion like an angel sings,
Still quiring to the young-eyed cherubins;
Such harmony is in immortal souls,
But whilst this muddy vesture of decay
Doth grossly close it in, we cannot hear it.
   Enter musicians
Come ho, and wake Diana with a hymn,
With sweetest touches pierce your mistress' ear
And draw her home with music.
   Music

JESSICA
   I am never merry when I hear sweet music.

LORENZO
   The reason is your spirits are attentive.   70
For do but note a wild and wanton herd
Or race of youthful and unhandled colts
Fetching mad bounds, bellowing and neighing loud,
Which is the hot condition of their blood,
If they but hear perchance a trumpet sound,
Or any air of music touch their ears,
You shall perceive them make a mutual stand,
Their savage eyes turned to a modest gaze
By the sweet power of music. Therefore the poet
Did feign that Orpheus drew trees, stones, and floods,   80
Since naught so stockish, hard, and full of rage
But music for the time doth change his nature.
The man that hath no music in himself,

Nor is not moved with concord of sweet sounds,
Is fit for treasons, stratagems, and spoils,
The motions of his spirit are dull as night,
And his affections dark as Erebus.
Let no such man be trusted. Mark the music.

Enter Portia and Nerissa

PORTIA

That light we see is burning in my hall;
How far that little candle throws his beams!
So shines a good deed in a naughty world.

NERISSA

When the moon shone we did not see the candle.

PORTIA

So doth the greater glory dim the less.
A substitute shines brightly as a king
Until a king be by, and then his state
Empties itself, as doth an inland brook
Into the main of waters. Music! hark!

NERISSA

It is your music, madam, of the house.

PORTIA

Nothing is good, I see, without respect;
Methinks it sounds much sweeter than by day.

NERISSA

Silence bestows that virtue on it, madam.

PORTIA

The crow doth sing as sweetly as the lark
When neither is attended, and I think
The nightingale, if she should sing by day
When every goose is cackling, would be thought
No better a musician than the wren.
How many things by season seasoned are
To their right praise and true perfection!
Peace!

Music ceases

How the moon sleeps with Endymion,
And would not be awaked.

LORENZO   That is the voice,   110
Or I am much deceived, of Portia.

PORTIA

He knows me as the blind man knows the cuckoo,
By the bad voice.

LORENZO   Dear lady, welcome home.

PORTIA

We have been praying for our husbands' welfare,
Which speed we hope the better for our words.
Are they returned?

LORENZO   Madam, they are not yet,
But there is come a messenger before
To signify their coming.

PORTIA   Go in, Nerissa,
Give order to my servants that they take
No note at all of our being absent hence,   120
Nor you, Lorenzo, Jessica, nor you.

A tucket sounds

LORENZO

Your husband is at hand, I hear his trumpet.
We are no tell-tales, madam; fear you not.

PORTIA

This night methinks is but the daylight sick,
It looks a little paler. 'Tis a day
Such as the day is when the sun is hid.

Enter Bassanio, Antonio, Gratiano, and their followers

BASSANIO

We should hold day with the Antipodes
If you would walk in absence of the sun.

PORTIA

Let me give light, but let me not be light,

130 For a light wife doth make a heavy husband,
And never be Bassanio so for me.
But God sort all! You are welcome home, my lord.

BASSANIO

I thank you, madam. Give welcome to my friend.
This is the man, this is Antonio,
To whom I am so infinitely bound.

PORTIA

You should in all sense be much bound to him,
For, as I hear, he was much bound for you.

ANTONIO

No more than I am well acquitted of.

PORTIA

Sir, you are very welcome to our house;
140 It must appear in other ways than words,
Therefore I scant this breathing courtesy.

GRATIANO (*to Nerissa*)

By yonder moon I swear you do me wrong!
In faith, I gave it to the judge's clerk.
Would he were gelt that had it for my part
Since you do take it, love, so much at heart.

PORTIA

A quarrel ho, already! What's the matter?

GRATIANO

About a hoop of gold, a paltry ring
That she did give me, whose posy was
For all the world like cutler's poetry
150 Upon a knife, 'Love me, and leave me not.'

NERISSA

What talk you of the posy or the value?
You swore to me when I did give it you
That you would wear it till your hour of death,
And that it should lie with you in your grave.
Though not for me, yet for your vehement oaths,

You should have been respective and have kept it.
Gave it a judge's clerk! No, God's my judge,
The clerk will ne'er wear hair on's face that had it!

GRATIANO

He will, an if he live to be a man.

NERISSA

Ay, if a woman live to be a man.   160

GRATIANO

Now by this hand, I gave it to a youth,
A kind of boy, a little scrubbèd boy
No higher than thyself, the judge's clerk,
A prating boy that begged it as a fee;
I could not for my heart deny it him.

PORTIA

You were to blame – I must be plain with you –
To part so slightly with your wife's first gift,
A thing stuck on with oaths upon your finger
And so riveted with faith unto your flesh.
I gave my love a ring, and made him swear   170
Never to part with it; and here he stands.
I dare be sworn for him he would not leave it
Nor pluck it from his finger for the wealth
That the world masters. Now in faith, Gratiano,
You give your wife too unkind a cause of grief.
An 'twere to me, I should be mad at it.

BASSANIO (aside)

Why, I were best to cut my left hand off
And swear I lost the ring defending it.

GRATIANO

My Lord Bassanio gave his ring away
Unto the judge that begged it, and indeed   180
Deserved it too; and then the boy, his clerk
That took some pains in writing, he begged mine,
And neither man nor master would take aught

But the two rings.

PORTIA   What ring gave you, my lord?
Not that, I hope, which you received of me?

BASSANIO
If I could add a lie unto a fault,
I would deny it, but you see my finger
Hath not the ring upon it, it is gone.

PORTIA
Even so void is your false heart of truth.
By heaven, I will ne'er come in your bed
Until I see the ring!

NERISSA   Nor I in yours
Till I again see mine!

BASSANIO   Sweet Portia,
If you did know to whom I gave the ring,
If you did know for whom I gave the ring,
And would conceive for what I gave the ring,
And how unwillingly I left the ring
When naught would be accepted but the ring,
You would abate the strength of your displeasure.

PORTIA
If you had known the virtue of the ring,
Or half her worthiness that gave the ring,
Or your own honour to contain the ring,
You would not then have parted with the ring.
What man is there so much unreasonable,
If you had pleased to have defended it
With any terms of zeal, wanted the modesty
To urge the thing held as a ceremony?
Nerissa teaches me what to believe,
I'll die for't but some woman had the ring!

BASSANIO
No, by my honour, madam! By my soul
No woman had it, but a civil doctor,

Which did refuse three thousand ducats of me
And begged the ring, the which I did deny him,
And suffered him to go displeased away,
Even he that had held up the very life
Of my dear friend. What should I say, sweet lady?
I was enforced to send it after him.
I was beset with shame and courtesy.
My honour would not let ingratitude
So much besmear it. Pardon me, good lady!
For by these blessèd candles of the night,   220
Had you been there I think you would have begged
The ring of me to give the worthy doctor.

PORTIA
Let not that doctor e'er come near my house.
Since he hath got the jewel that I loved,
And that which you did swear to keep for me,
I will become as liberal as you,
I'll not deny him anything I have,
No, not my body nor my husband's bed.
Know him I shall, I am well sure of it.
Lie not a night from home; watch me like Argus.   230
If you do not, if I be left alone,
Now by mine honour which is yet mine own,
I'll have that doctor for my bedfellow.

NERISSA
And I his clerk. Therefore be well advised
How you do leave me to mine own protection.

GRATIANO
Well, do you so. Let not me take him then!
For if I do, I'll mar the young clerk's pen.

ANTONIO
I am th'unhappy subject of these quarrels.

PORTIA
Sir, grieve not you, you are welcome notwithstanding.

BASSANIO

240   Portia, forgive me this enforcèd wrong,
And in the hearing of these many friends
I swear to thee, even by thine own fair eyes,
Wherein I see myself . . .

PORTIA   Mark you but that!
In both my eyes he doubly sees himself,
In each eye one. Swear by your double self,
And there's an oath of credit.

BASSANIO   Nay, but hear me.
Pardon this fault, and by my soul I swear
I never more will break an oath with thee.

ANTONIO

I once did lend my body for his wealth,
250   Which but for him that had your husband's ring
Had quite miscarried. I dare be bound again,
My soul upon the forfeit, that your lord
Will never more break faith advisedly.

PORTIA

Then you shall be his surety. Give him this,
And bid him keep it better than the other.

ANTONIO

Here, Lord Bassanio. Swear to keep this ring.

BASSANIO

By heaven, it is the same I gave the doctor!

PORTIA

I had it of him. Pardon me, Bassanio,
For by this ring the doctor lay with me.

NERISSA

260   And pardon me, my gentle Gratiano,
For that same scrubbèd boy, the doctor's clerk,
In lieu of this last night did lie with me.

GRATIANO

Why, this is like the mending of highways

In summer, where the ways are fair enough.
What, are we cuckolds ere we have deserved it?

PORTIA
Speak not so grossly. You are all amazed.
Here is a letter, read it at your leisure.
It comes from Padua from Bellario.
There you shall find that Portia was the doctor,
Nerissa there her clerk. Lorenzo here   270
Shall witness I set forth as soon as you,
And even but now returned, I have not yet
Entered my house. Antonio, you are welcome,
And I have better news in store for you
Than you expect. Unseal this letter soon,
There you shall find three of your argosies
Are richly come to harbour suddenly.
You shall not know by what strange accident
I chancèd on this letter.

ANTONIO   I am dumb!

BASSANIO
Were you the doctor and I knew you not?   280

GRATIANO
Were you the clerk that is to make me cuckold?

NERISSA
Ay, but the clerk that never means to do it,
Unless he live until he be a man.

BASSANIO
Sweet doctor, you shall be my bedfellow.
When I am absent, then lie with my wife.

ANTONIO
Sweet lady, you have given me life and living,
For here I read for certain that my ships
Are safely come to road.

PORTIA   How now, Lorenzo?
My clerk hath some good comforts too for you.

NERISSA

290   Ay, and I'll give them him without a fee.
There do I give to you and Jessica
From the rich Jew, a special deed of gift,
After his death, of all he dies possessed of.

LORENZO

Fair ladies, you drop manna in the way
Of starvèd people.

PORTIA   It is almost morning,
And yet I am sure you are not satisfied
Of these events at full. Let us go in,
And charge us there upon inter'gatories,
And we will answer all things faithfully.

GRATIANO

300   Let it be so. The first inter'gatory
That my Nerissa shall be sworn on is
Whether till the next night she had rather stay,
Or go to bed now, being two hours to day.
But were the day come, I should wish it dark
Till I were couching with the doctor's clerk.
Well, while I live I'll fear no other thing
So sore as keeping safe Nerissa's ring.   *Exeunt*

An Account of the Text

The first known mention of Shakespeare's play is an entry on 22 July 1598 in the Stationers' Register of books authorized for publication. A printer called James Roberts entered 'a book of the Merchant of Venice, or Otherwise Called the Jew of Venice'. Two years later (1600) appeared 'The most excellent Historie of the *Merchant of Venice*. With the extreame crueltie of *Shylocke* the Iewe towards the sayd Merchant, in cutting a iust pound of his flesh: and the obtayning of *Portia* by the choyse of three chests. *As it hath beene diuers times acted by the Lord Chamberlaine his Seruants*. Written by William Shakespeare.' The title given on the first page of the text and in the running heads at the top of each pair of pages is 'The comicall History of the Merchant of Venice'. We have no reason to suppose that these descriptions of the play are Shakespeare's; they sound more like the printer's inventions.

This first edition of the play (which we refer to as Q1) was printed probably from a manuscript that was close to Shakespeare's. It may have been his own rough manuscript which was kept as a working copy in the playhouse. Two of the stage directions are in an imperative form ('open the letter', III.2.236; and 'play Musique', V.1.68) and perhaps indicate the closeness of the text to the playhouse prompt book.

Q1 is our only authority for the text of the play. It was reprinted in 1619 by William Jaggard but the date of the original edition (1600) and the name of the original printer (James Roberts) were falsely kept on the title page (this edition is referred to as Q2). It makes a few obvious corrections of errors in Q1, as well as introducing new errors of its own. The play was reprinted in the Folio edition of Shakespeare's plays in 1623 (referred to as F). The printer of the Folio used Q1 as his copy; some corrections were made and some new errors introduced. There is no reason to suppose that the changes in Q2 and in F had the author's approval; they were probably more or less intelligent guesses made in the printing house.

COLLATIONS

The following lists are *selective*. They include the more important and interesting variants. Minor changes which are not disputed, small variations in word order, obvious misprints and grammatical corrections not affecting the sense are not generally included here. A few modernizations of spelling which substantially alter the form of the word are also included.

l

The following readings in the present text of *The Merchant of Venice* are emendations of the words found in Q1 (which are placed afterwards in the original spelling, with where appropriate the forms found in other early texts). A few of the alterations were made in the printing of Q2 (1619), or in the Folios F (1623), F2 (1632), F3 (1663–4), F4 (1685). Most of the other emendations were made by the eighteenth-century editors.

I.1

13 curtsy] cursie Q1, Q2; curtsie F

19 Peering] F; Piring Q1; Piering Q2

27 Andrew docked] *Andrew* docks Q1, F; *Andrew* dockes Q2

84 alabaster] Alablaster

I.2

43 County Palatine] Q2; Countie Palentine Q1, F

51–2 Le Bon] *Le Boune*

56 Count Palatine] Q2; Count Palentine Q1, F

57 throstle] Trassell Q1, Q2, F

I.3

47 well-won] Q2; well-wone Q1; well-worne F

75 compromised] compremyzd Q1, Q2; compremyz'd F
131 breed of] F; breede for Q1, Q2
    barren] Q2; barraine Q1, F

II.1

31 thee, lady] the Lady
35 page] rage Q1, Q2, F

II.2

3 (*and elsewhere*) Gobbo] Q2; Iobbe Q1, F

II.3

11 did] F2; doe Q1, Q2, F

II.7

69 *tombs*] *timber*

II.8

39 Slubber] Q2, F; slumber

III.1

27 fledged] Q2; flidge Q1; fledg'd F
45 courtesy] cursie Q1; curtsie Q2, F
97 Heard] heere

III.2

67 eyes] F; eye
81 vice] F2; voyce Q1; voice Q2, F
93 make] maketh Q1, Q2; makes F
101 Therefore thou] Therefore then thou
204 roof] Q2; rough Q1, F

III.4

49 Padua] Mantua
50 cousin's hand] F; cosin hands Q1; Cosins hands Q2
53 traject] Tranect Q1, Q2, F

III.5

20 e'en] Q2, F; in Q1
72–3 merit it, | In] meane it, it | in Q1; meane it, then |
     In Q2; meane it, it | In F
79 for a wife] for wife

IV.1

30 his state] Q2, F; this states Q1
51 Master] Maisters Q1, Q2; Masters F
74 bleat] F; bleake Q1, Q2
75 mountain] mountaine of
100 'tis] Q2, F; as Q1

150 CLERK] *not in* Q1, Q2, F *and so presumably attributed to the Duke*

V.I

49 Sweet soul] *as the last words of Launcelot's previous
speech in* Q1, Q2, F

51 Stephano] Q2; *Stephen* Q1, F

233 my] Q2, F; mine Q1

2

The following are some of the more interesting and important
variant readings and proposed emendations *not* accepted in the
present text of *The Merchant of Venice*. Many of these rejected
readings will be found in older editions (especially of the nineteenth century).

The reading of this edition (which derives from Q1 unless otherwise stated) is given first, followed by the rejected variants. If a
source of the variant is not given, the reading is an emendation
by an editor (most of them are of the eighteenth century).

I.1

10 on] of

I.2

6–7 mean happiness] smal happinesse F

30–31 one who you shall] one who shall Q2, F

72 Scottish] Q1, Q2; other F

I.3

22–3 water thieves and land thieves] land thieves and
water thieves

62 ye would] he would haue Q2; he would F; we would

131 barren] bearing

II.1

18 wit] will

35 page] rage Q1, Q2, F; rogue (*C. J. Sisson*); wag
(*J. Dover Wilson*)

II.2

155–6 the twinkling] the twinkling of an eye Q2

II.4

5 us] as F4

II.6

14 younger] younker

II.9

78 wroth] wroath Q1, Q2, F; wrath, ruth, roth (= *ruth*)

III.1

97 Heard] heere Q1; here; where?

III.4

106 paleness] plainness
158 sum of something] sum of nothing F

IV.1

56 woollen] wauling
128 inexecrable] inexorable F3
150 CLERK] *not in* Q1, Q2, F; NERISSA (*C. J. Sisson*)
256 Is it so] It is not F

V.1

41–2 Master Lorenzo? Master Lorenzo!] M. Lorenzo, & M. Lorenzo Q1; Master Lorenzo and Mistress Lorenzo?
109 Peace! *Music ceases* How] Peace, how Q1; Peace, ho!

3 Stage Directions

The stage directions of the present edition are based on those of the Quartos of 1600 and 1619, and the first Folio. Some of the original directions have simply been regularized. For instance, at the beginning of II.2 the Quarto's '*Enter the Clowne alone*' has been altered to '*Enter Launcelot Gobbo, alone*'. Similarly, instructions for actions obviously demanded by the text have been added: '*He looks at his palm*' (II.2.146) is an instance. When the Quarto text was reprinted in the Folio the principal changes in the stage directions were of additional directions for flourishes of cornets. These have been incorporated. The following list includes the more interesting changes from the first Quarto. Q indicates both Quartos.

II.1

0 *Flourish of cornets*] *not in* Q; *Flo. Cornets* F
46 *Flourish of cornets. Exeunt*] *Exeunt* Q; *Cornets. Exeunt* F

II.2

72 (*He kneels*)] *not in* Q, F
104 *Enter Bassanio, with Leonardo and a follower or two*]

Enter Bassanio *with a follower or two* Q, F

108 *Exit one of his men*] Q2; *not in* Q1, F

156 *Exit Launcelot, with Old Gobbo*] *Exit Clowne* Q, F

II.4

9 *with a letter*] *with a Letter* F; *not in* Q

II.6

25 *Enter Jessica above, in boy's clothes*] *Iessica aboue* Q, F

50 *Exit above*] *not in* Q, F

57 *Enter Jessica below*] Enter *Iessica* Q, F

59 *Exit with Jessica and Salerio*] *Exit* Q, F

II.7

0, 77 *Flourish of cornets*] *not in* Q; *Flo. Cornets* F (*after* 'Enter Salarino and Solanio' (II.8.0), *probably accidentally misplaced from* II.7.77. *It seems likely that Morocco's entry as well as his exit would have been signalled by a flourish*)

II.9

3 *Flourish of cornets*] *not in* Q; *Flor. Cornets* F

78 *Exit with his train*] *not in* Q, F

III.3

0 *Solanio*] F; *Salerio* Q1; *Salarino* Q

IV.1

0 *Salerio, and Gratiano with others*] *and Gratiano* Q, F

118 *dressed like a lawyer's clerk*] *not in* Q, F

120 *She presents a letter*] *not in* Q, F

163 *dressed like a Doctor of Laws*] *not in* Q, F

423 *Bassanio takes off his gloves*] *not in* Q, F

IV.2

0 *Enter Portia and Nerissa, disguised as before*] Enter *Nerrissa* Q; *Enter Portia and Nerissa* F

V.1

65 *Enter musicians*] *not in* Q, F

109 *Music ceases*] F; *not in* Q

121 *A tucket sounds*] F; *not in* Q

Commentary

The Merchant of Venice contains a large number of biblical allusions. In these notes they are cited from the version that Shakespeare would hear in church, the Bishops' Bible. This was first published in 1568, and was the official translation in the English Church until its replacement by the King James version of 1611. At certain points the Geneva translation, made by English Protestant exiles during the reign of Mary and first published at Geneva in 1560, has also been quoted to illustrate an interesting verbal parallel. Shakespeare may have read this version. All biblical quotations are given in modernized spelling.

The Title: The Quarto of 1600 (Q1) title page has 'The most excellent Historie of the *Merchant of Venice*', with running heads 'The comicall History of | the Merchant of Venice'. The Quarto of 1619 (Q2) amends slightly to 'The Excellent History of the Merchant of Venice' on the title page, retaining the running heads of Q1. The Folio of 1623 (F) has simply 'The Merchant of Venice'. George Granville (Lord Lansdowne) published his adaptation in 1701 as 'The Jew of Venice. A Comedy'.

I.1

    0 *Salerio, and Solanio*: Q2 lists three characters *Solanio*, *Salarino*, and *Salerio*. *Salarino* appears to have been a mere reduplication (perhaps with additional confusion through abbreviated speech-prefixes) of *Salerio*.

    1 *I know not why I am so sad*: Antonio's unexplained melancholy has been given many explanations: that

it is a relic of an earlier version adapted by Shakespeare; that it is due to the imminent parting with
Bassanio; that (a frequent explanation) it is a fore-
boding of the play's 'tragedy'; that melancholy is
'a malady of the rich', 'made blunt and effeminate'
by luxury; that this *want-wit* melancholy is a necessary preparation for the inexplicable levity of a *royal
merchant*, normally wise and prudent, in signing such
a bond as Shylock proposes.

7 *know myself*: A version of the aphorism '*Nosce teipsum*',
an Elizabethan commonplace and the subject of a
poem by Sir John Davies in 1599.

9 *argosies*: From the Italian '*una nave ragusea*', a Venetian
vessel, with perhaps, by false derivation, a punning
allusion to the ship *Argo* (cf. *golden fleece* below).
Ragusa is in fact the modern Dubrovnik on the
Adriatic coast.

portly: Majestic.

11 *pageants*: The large set-pieces in the forms of ships,
castles, etc., were drawn about the streets in shows
and pageants.

12 *overpeer*: Look down upon.

13 *curtsy*: Qs give *cursie*, F *curtsie*. The bobbing motion
of a small vessel in the wake of a larger.

15 *venture*: The first suggestion, to be intensified later
to its climax in Shylock's caustic *ventures . . . squandered abroad* in scene 3, of the risk or gamble involved
in foreign trade.

19 *roads*: Anchorages.

26 *flats*: Shoals. Cf. the reference to the Goodwins in
III.I.4.

27 *Andrew*: This has been explained as a reference to
an Italian naval commander, Andrea Doria, and to
a Spanish galleon, the *St Andrew*, captured at Cadiz
in 1596.

28 *Vailing*: Giving sign of submission.

29 *burial*: Burial place.

42 *bottom*: Ship's hold.

50 *Janus*: The two-countenanced deity, god of exits and

entrances, celebrated in the opening month of the calendar. There is no evidence from effigies on coins or in sculpture that the two heads differed in mood, and Shakespeare (followed by all his editors) probably conflates Janus with the double masks of comedy and tragedy.

52 *peep*: Laugh with half-closed eyes.

56 *Nestor*: The oldest of the heroes, the type of wisdom and gravity.

Gratiano: The name Graziano appears to have been the name for the comic *dottore* in *commedia dell'arte*. He takes it upon himself both to 'play the fool' and to make quasi-medical judgements on his friends throughout the first scene.

60 *made you merry*: Burton, in the *Anatomy of Melancholy* (1621), declares the best cure for melancholy (like Antonio's) is 'a cup of strong drink, mirth, music, and merry company'.

61 *prevented*: Anticipated, gone before.

67 *strange*: Distant.

74 *respect upon*: Regard for.

75 *They lose it that do buy it with much care.* Cf. Matthew 16:25: 'whosoever will save his life, shall lose it.'

77–8 *world . . . | A stage*: Cf. Jaques in *As You Like It*, II.7.140: 'All the world's a stage . . .'

79 *fool*: Gratiano may, like Launcelot later, be cast in the analogy of the buffoon; see note on 56 above.

81–2 *liver . . . heart*: The liver was coupled with the heart and brain, as the vital organs of the body; the supposed seat of love and violent passion. Cf. *Cymbeline*, V.5.14–15: 'To you, the liver, heart, and brain of Britain, | By whom I grant she lives.' Sighs and groans were thought to drain blood from the heart; see *Romeo and Juliet*, III.5.59: 'Dry sorrow drinks our blood'; and *A Midsummer Night's Dream*, III.2.97: 'sighs of love, that costs the fresh blood dear'.

84 *grandsire cut in alabaster*: The Q line, here repunctuated, reads *Sit like his grandsire, cut in Alablaster?*

Memorial tablets and tombs in churches are frequently in alabaster, a sensitive stone for carving. The Q spelling *Alablaster* is common, by confusion with 'arblaster' a crossbow man, also spelt 'alablaster'.

85 *jaundice*: Yellowness of the skin caused by obstruction of the bile; commonly thought to be excited by 'the more violent mental emotions'. Cf. *Troilus and Cressida*, I.3.2: 'What grief hath set the jaundice on your cheeks?'

88 *sort*: Kind; band.

89 *cream and mantle*: Cover with a pale and sour froth. Cf. *King Lear*, III.4.127: 'the green mantle of the standing pool'.

92 *conceit*: Conception, understanding.

93 *Sir Oracle*: F has *Sir an oracle*, punctuated by Granville, *Jew of Venice*, 'I am, Sir, an Oracle.' But see *The Winter's Tale*, I.2.196: 'Sir Smile, his neighbour'.

96–7 *reputed wise | For saying nothing*: See Proverbs 17:28: 'Even a fool, when he holdeth his tongue, is counted wise.'

99 *call their brothers fools*: See Matthew 5:22: 'whosoever shall say [to his brother] thou fool, shall be in danger of hell fire.'

102 *gudgeon*: A freshwater fish – *Gobio fluviatilis* – used as bait; a gullible person.

104 *after dinner*: As the Puritan divines continued their long sermons.

110 *gear*: Business; or, perhaps better, nonsense-talk.

112 *neat's tongue*: Ox tongue.
      not vendible: Not marriageable.

120 *pilgrimage*: The lover is exalted almost to canonization; cf. II.7.40: *To kiss this shrine, this mortal breathing saint.*

124 *something*: Somewhat.
      port: Style.

129 *time*: Young lifetime.

130 *gaged*: Pledged, as in pawn. A first anticipation of the bond plot.

132 *warranty*: Authorization. A legal term (a covenant

or undertaking in contract), extending the implication of 'gage', as an anticipation of the bond.

137 *eye of honour*: Scope of honour's vision.

141 *of the self-same flight*: Of the same trajectory, size or weight, equally feathered.

142 *advisèd*: Deliberate.

145 *pure innocence*: The guilelessness of the *childhood proof* in the previous line.

150–51 *or . . . | Or*: Either . . . or.

154 *To wind about my love with circumstance*: To beat about the bush. *circumstance* means circumlocution.

160 *prest*: Ready. From Old French and the popular Latin *'praestus'* (modern French *'prêt'*); there is probably an overtone of 'pressed', meaning 'bound', again carrying a premonition of the bond plot.

162 *fair*: This adjective begins the series continued in *sunny* and *golden*. Portia is conceived as the ideal of the Venetian school of painting, of Titian and Giorgione, of a fair, red-gold hair, the colour with which Queen Elizabeth qualified as a fair beauty (as opposed to the 'dark lady'). Emphasizing the contrast, Nerissa's name appears derived from the Italian *'Nericcia'* (from *'nero'*, black[-haired]). Portia is of course in the Petrarchan tradition; like Petrarch's Laura, she has *'biondi capelli'*, *'cape' d'oro'*, *'le treccie bionde Ch'oro forbito e perle Eran . . . a vederle'* ('fair hair', 'a golden head', 'fair tresses which resembled rich gold and pearls').

165–6 *Portia . . . Cato's daughter, Brutus' Portia*: Shakespeare appears to have intended her name to carry considerable significance. It is possible that there is a light pun on 'portion', with its implication of 'inheritance' or 'dowry'. Portia, wife of Marcus Junius Brutus, conspirator with Cassius against Caesar, was the daughter of Cato Uticensis, who had gained a particular reputation for rectitude and was himself an enemy of Caesar's. Cf. *Julius Caesar*, II.1.296–7: 'Think you I am no stronger than my sex, | Being so fathered, and so husbanded?'

170 *golden fleece*: Jason gathered the Argonauts who
    sought the Golden Fleece, finding it in Colchis and
    winning it with the aid of Medea, the enchantress-
    daughter of the King of Colchis; the latter, like
    Portia's father, confronted the Argonauts with a triple
    test of their wit. Medea appears again in the play
    (V.1.13–14), when she *did renew old Aeson*, the father
    of Jason. Cf. III.2.241: 'We are the Jasons, we have
    won the Fleece.'

171 *strond*: Strand, shore.

175 *thrift*: Bassanio's quest is conceived in terms which
    link him with the Shylock/Laban 'way to thrive',
    for *thrift is blessing if men steal it not* (I.3.87).

181 *racked*: Strained. With its associations with 'rack-
    rent' and with the instrument of torture, this passage
    emphasizes the darker aspect of Bassanio's squan-
    dering dependence on Antonio, which was hinted at
    at 157, *Than if you had made waste of all I have.*
    Both Bassanio and Antonio earn the austere Shylock's
    contempt as *prodigals*, with *ventures . . . squandered
    abroad.*

183 *presently*: Immediately.

I.2

0 *Nerissa*: This name is probably derived from the
    Italian implying dark-haired (see note on I.1.162),
    by contrast with the golden Portia.

1 *aweary*: Portia opens the first scene in the more
    golden world of Belmont with an echo of Antonio's
    malaise in the first scene in Venice.

7–9 *superfluity comes sooner by white hairs, but competency
    lives longer*: Excess ages sooner but moderation lives
    longer.

10 *sentences*: Sententiae, aphorisms. With perhaps a light
    pun on the legal sense.
    pronounced: Delivered. This extends the legal phrase-
    ology – perhaps preparing for Portia's role in Act
    IV – through her next speeches, with *laws, decree,
    counsel, surety, sealed under.*

13 *chapels had been churches*: A chapel is frequently a

portion of a large church, often separately dedicated and with its own altar; the term was also used for an outlying chapel of a principal church or monastery. Cf. its use in Stratford for the Guild Chapel.

21–7 *choose . . . will . . . lottery*: A complex pun extends Portia's dilemma through these lines: her father's *will* (i.e. both 'choice' and 'testament') limits her personal choice; the element of chance or apparent caprice in the casket device, meriting the term 'lottery', is modified by the pun implied in that word on 'allottery'. Cf. *As You Like It*, I.1.68 – where Orlando's inheritance is described as 'the poor allottery my father left me by testament'.

36 *level at*: Aim at.

37 *Neapolitan*: The Neapolitans of Shakespeare's day were especially famed for horsemanship.

38 *colt*: Callow, uncouth young man.

43 *County Palatine*: Count occasionally (but see 56) retains the second syllable of the French and Italian forms. The daughter of James I married a Count Palatine.

46–7 *weeping philosopher*: Heraclitus of Ephesus, (*c.* 500 BC). Juvenal, satirizing the 'vanity of human wishes', contrasts the laughing philosopher, Democritus, with the weeping philosopher Heraclitus (*Satire X*, 31–2).

48–9 *death's-head*: A memento mori; a 'skull and crossed bones' frequently engraved on brasses or cut on tombstones.

57 *throstle*: Thrush (*trassell* in Q and F, probably a dialect pronunciation).

69 *How oddly he is suited! . . .*: Cf. Robert Greene, *Farewell to Follie* (1591): 'I have seen an English gentleman so diffused in his suits, his doublet being for the wear of Castile, his hose for Venice, his hat for France, his cloak for Germany'; and Thomas Nashe's English youth in *The Unfortunate Traveller* (1594), who 'imitated four or five sundry nations in my attire at once'.

70 *round hose*: Circular or puffed-out hose.

72 *Scottish*: This is the Q reading; it is assumed that
    the F emendation to *other lord* reflects the wish for
    better relations with Scotland after James's acces-
    sion.

76–7 *the Frenchman became his surety*: Reference to the
    'auld alliance' between Scotland and France, a con-
    stant trouble to Elizabeth. Note Portia's legal terms
    relating to bonds and sureties.

83–4 *best . . . beast*: Punningly.

90 *Rhenish*: Cf. III.1.37, where Rhenish is preferred to
    red wine (a judgement echoed in part in *King Lear*,
    I.1.258, in France's derogatory 'waterish Burgundy').
    William Turner, describing wine drunk in England
    in 1568, says that 'Rhenish wine . . . is commonly
    a year old at the least, before it be drunken: and
    therefore it is older [and more potent] than the
    common claret wine, which dureth not commonly
    above one year'.

98 *imposition*: Command, will.

100 *Sibylla*: A proper name (as opposed to the 'nine sibyls'
    of *Henry VI, Part I*, I.2.56) and hence the Cumaean
    Sibyl of Ovid, *Metamorphoses*, XIV, who asked
    Apollo for the gift of long life.

101 *Diana*: 'Queen and huntress, chaste and fair' (Ben
    Jonson, 'Hymn to Diana' from *Cynthia's Revels*
    (1601)). Cf. *Henry IV, Part I*, I.2.25–6: 'let us be
    Diana's foresters . . . minions of the moon'; and *A
    Midsummer Night's Dream*, I.1.89–90: 'on Diana's
    altar to protest | For aye austerity and single life'.

107 *a scholar and a soldier*: Cf. Ophelia's ideal 'noble mind'
    (*Hamlet*, III.1.151–2): 'The courtier's, soldier's,
    scholar's, eye, tongue, sword'.

108 *Marquis of Montferrat*: Nerissa could scarcely cite a
    more evocative family name for the scholar-soldier
    companion to Bassanio. The house of Monferrato
    was founded in 967 and for centuries struggled with
    Savoy for the leadership of Lombardy; it was a
    leading power throughout the Crusades and in 1175

inherited the kingdom of Thessalonica, a key city in the amber trade with Venice. William the Great of Monferrato in 1257 married Isabella, daughter of the Duke of Gloucester; he established an alliance with the Visconti of Milan and was the virtual creator of the *condottieri*. The family declined in the fifteenth century and by the mid sixteenth century the marquisate passed to the Dukes of Mantua.

109 *Yes, yes, it was Bassanio*: Portia answers impetuously and immediately covers up her eagerness.

124 *complexion of a devil*: Cf. *Othello*, V.2.132: 'And you the blacker devil'.

125–7 *Come, Nerissa . . . door*: A very rough doggerel 'couplet' closing the scene.

1.3

0 *Shylock*: There are many suggestions for the derivation of the name, of which the principal are: (1) from the Hebrew 'Shallach', a cormorant, a frequent Elizabethan term for usurers; (2) from an obscure dialect word 'shallock', to idle or slouch. More attractive is the suggestion that it is a semi-morality term, Shy-Lock, implying secrecy and hoarding. But the name was also used in English, meaning 'white-haired', equivalent to Whitlock or Whitehead. See Introduction, p. xxxv.

1 *ducats*: A ducat (literally, a piece coined by a duke or doge) is a Venetian gold piece, *Ducatus Venetorum*, worth, depending on the exchange rate, between 8 and 11 shillings (40–55p). As a rough guide, two ducats to the pound is a reasonable estimate. By any calculation of values, then, the sum of 3,000 ducats was enormous, approximately £1,500 at a time when the annual salary for Stratford's schoolmaster was £20, Shakespeare bought New Place, one of Stratford's largest houses, for £60 and Sir Andrew Aguecheek in *Twelfth Night* had an annual income of 3,000 ducats. Exact calculations of the modern value are impossible but the loan represents a sum of not less than £375,000. See Introduction, pp. xxvii–xxviii.

1, 6 *well*: This is assent and not a question, as some editors have suggested.

   7 *stead*: 'Assist' or 'supply'.

  12 *a good man*: A dramatic ambiguity; Shylock opens up the possibility of misunderstanding which he tactically withdraws when Bassanio is roused. Cf. *Coriolanus*, I.1.14–15: 'We are accounted poor citizens, the patricians good.'

  17 *sufficient*: Adequate surety.
     supposition: Doubt.

  19 *Rialto*: Both the bridge (the Ponte di Rialto) and the Exchange or Bourse – 'an eminent place in Venice where merchants commonly meet' (John Florio, *Italian Dictionary* (1611)).

  21 *squandered*: The verb emphasizes the suggestion of prodigality in Shylock's *ventures* in the previous line, as it also continues his ambiguous manner, for 'squander' may mean scatter, with no pejorative meaning.

  23 *pirates*: But Q and F have *Pyrats*, sardonically extending *land rats and water rats* in the previous line.

27–8 *assured*: A further sardonic emphasis, shifting the meaning from Bassanio's 'certain' to Shylock's 'guaranteed'.

  32 *prophet the Nazarite*: Both Jews and Mohammedans conceded the prophetic, though not the divine, status of Christ. Nazarite is a false etymology; properly it was a prophet under special vows (for example, Samson and John the Baptist); but in all the English translations of the Bible until 1611 it was used falsely for 'Nazarene', an inhabitant of Nazareth.
     conjured the devil into: The miracle of the Gadarene swine in Matthew 8, Mark 5 and Luke 8.

34–5 *I will not eat with you, drink with you, nor pray with you*: Eating and drinking are for Shylock sacramental acts and his religious exclusiveness is equally conveyed in the three verbs.

  38 *fawning publican*: A vividly unusual term for the *publicani*, the renegade Jewish taxgatherers employed

by ancient Rome. Two senses fit Shylock's use: his
contempt for the penitent publican in the parable of
Luke 18 who desired mercy; his identification of
Antonio with the oppressive publicans who robbed
the Jews of *well-won thrift*.

42–8 *usance . . . thrift . . . interest*: The variety of terms
corresponds to degrees of reprehension and excuse
for a hated practice. William Thomas, *Historye of
Italye* (1561), describes the wealth of the Venetian
Jews through usury: 'It is almost incredible what
gain the Venetians receive by the usury of the Jews
. . . by reason whereof the Jews are out of measure
wealthy in those parts.' Francis Bacon's *Essay of
Usury* (1625) declares both 'that it is against nature
for money to beget money' and that 'Usurers should
have orange-tawny bonnets because they do Judaize',
a pun on Judas and Judah, with a dual reference to
the Judas-colour and the yellow cap of the Jewish
dress in some parts of Christendom.

43 *upon the hip*: A wrestling term with a possible reference to the dislocation of Jacob's hip in wrestling with
the angel in Genesis 32.

44–8 *ancient grudge . . . sacred nation . . . my tribe*: This
is the emotional key to the relationship between
Shylock and Antonio. Religious and racial pride
precede commercial rivalry.

54 *Tubal*: This is clearly a biblical name, associated
with Tubal-cain, a maker of instruments or weapons.
The name may also have associations with alien or
outcast peoples; this brings him into appropriate
association with Chus (or Cush): *his* [Shylock's] *countrymen* (III.2.285). Cush has certainly alien overtones, for it is the land of Ethiopia.

59 *excess*: Another pejorative word for usury, echoed
by Shylock in *advantage* at 67 and taken up into the
Belmont scenes in Portia's *scant this excess* (III.2.112).

60 *ripe*: Furness conjectured 'rife wants', wants that come
thick upon him. Johnson: 'wants that can have no
longer delay'.

61 *possessed*: Informed. Cf. *Twelfth Night*, II.3.133: 'Possess us, possess us'.

68–71 *Jacob . . . wise mother . . . third possessor*: This is a complex passage paraphrasing a great deal in Genesis 27 and 30. Esau should have inherited from Isaac and would therefore have been *The third possessor* after Abraham; but Rebekah, Jacob's *wise mother*, conspired with Jacob to cheat his blind father Isaac both of his blessing and Esau's inheritance, by putting 'the skins of kids upon his hands and upon the smooth of his neck' (27:16). Shylock's savouring of Jacob's being *The third possessor* is both pride in his own lineage and a sardonic approval of sharp practice. Shakespeare and his contemporary readers of the Bible would be clear about the orthodox attitude to the incident, for the Geneva Bible has a marginal comment that 'this subtilty is blameworthy because [Rebekah] should have tarried till God had performed his promise' and the Bishops' Bible (which Shakespeare appears to have used most often) that 'Jacob was not without fault, who might have tarried until God had changed his father's mind.'

75–85 *When Laban and himself were compromised . . . Jacob's*: These eleven lines describe Jacob's further dubious treatment of his father-in-law Laban, and anticipate Shylock's trick with the bond. The passage echoes the language of the Bishops' Bible ('and the sheep conceived before the rods and brought forth lambs ring-straked, spotted and partie' (Genesis 30:39)), but the clash between Antonio and Shylock on the ambiguous morality of Jacob's action is reflected in the strained marginal glosses: the Geneva Bible has the comment, 'Jacob herein used no deceit: for it was God's commandment' that Jacob should thrive; the Bishops' Bible is even more uneasy. 'All the increase of our labour is to be looked for at God's hand' but 'it is not lawful by fraud to seek recompense of injury:' (which Laban had done to Jacob) 'therefore Moses sheweth afterwards (Genesis 31:5) that God thus instructed Jacob'. In the whole of this passage Shakespeare shows a striking insight into the Jewish pride in race, and a remarkable command of biblical and theological argument.

75 *compromised*: In agreement.

76 *eanlings*: New-born lambs (from Old English '*eanian*', to give birth).

82 *kind*: Nature.

86–7 *thrive . . . thrift*: Shylock describes Jacob's sharp practice in the language of thrift which was used by the Puritans to account for their worldly success through moral uprightness.

88 *venture*: Antonio's riposte to Shylock's *ventures . . . squandered* (20–21).

99 *goodly outside*: The contrast between appearance and reality is a Shakespearian commonplace; it is central to the casket scenes later.

106 *patient shrug*: Often seen at the time as a semitic gesture; cf. *The Jew of Malta*, II.3.24: 'Heave up my shoulder when they call me dog'.

107 *badge*: The literal significance is much debated; Booth wrote in his published acting-version: 'I prefer the yellow cap [Bacon's 'orange-tawny bonnet'] to the cross upon the shoulder which other actors have worn, my Father among them. Cooke used the cap, and said that Macklin also used it.' (See note on 109.)

108 *misbeliever*: A very precise term. A Jew was not an *un*believer, an atheist or an infidel, but a *mis*believer, one who believes wrongly or heretically. See the Collect for Good Friday, recited until recently in varying forms in both the Anglican and the Roman use: 'Have mercy upon all Jews, Turks, Infidels, and Heretics.'

109 *Jewish gaberdine*: Vecellio's treatise on costume (1590) makes no distinction in the dress of Jew and Christian except the yellow cap; the *gavardina* was simply a peasant's cloak. Stage tradition may be echoed in Jordan's ballad *The Forfeiture* (1664):

> His habit was a Jewish gown,
> That would defend all weather;

for after 1412 all Moors and Jews in Spain had to wear such a long cloak, which came to their feet.

120 *bondman*: Cf. *purchased slave* in the trial scene, IV.1.90.

131 *breed of barren metal*: Q has *breede for*. Commentators have boggled at the antithesis *breed–barren*, Theobald suggesting 'bearing metal' and Pope 'bribe of . . .' Lord Lansdowne's *The Jew of Venice* (1701) has 'A Breed of sordid Mettal'. The passage in fact reflected the normal attitude of the playwrights to usury, that it was 'against nature'.

137 *doit*: A trifle; a Dutch coin (*'duit'*) 'whereof eight go to a stiver, and ten stivers do make our English shilling' (Thomas Coryat (1611)).

139 *This is kind I offer*: *kind* is a pun on its two possible meanings, the noun 'nature' and the adjective 'generous'.

141 *notary*: A clerk specifically authorized to draw up contracts.

142 *single bond*: This seems to imply a *simplex obligatio*, a promise to pay without conditions attached. But this bond is precisely different, has conditions annexed and Shylock would appear to be deceitfully playing down its graver implications to the level of his *merry sport*.

146 *nominated for*: Named as.
equal pound: Precise or just weight. This ironically prepares for Portia's quibble: *nor cut thou less nor more | But just a pound of flesh* (IV.1.322–3).

147 *fair flesh*: Possibly an ironic contrast between the fair Venetian and the darker, oriental Shylock.

171 *purse the ducats straight*: At the beginning of the scene Shylock purported to depend on Tubal for part of the sum.

175 *The Hebrew will turn Christian*: A climax of irony

in an ironic scene, anticipating the judgment on Shylock.

kind: A final use of the pun, several times repeated in this scene, playing on 'kindness' and 'nature'.

178 *My ships come home*: A hubristic tempting of chance and fate, the venture which Shylock despised.

II.1

0 *the Prince of Morocco, a tawny Moor*: Shakespeare portrays two other moors, Aaron in *Titus Andronicus* and Othello. In all three characters there is a concern with the dark skin, but in *The Merchant of Venice* and *Othello* the moor is a figure of conscious dignity and nobility. Morocco was a tawny moor as opposed to a 'blackamoor'. Cf. Aaron (*Titus Andronicus*, V.1.27), who is a 'tawny slave', and Raleigh's phrase 'The Negro's which we call the Blacke-Mores'.

accordingly: Matching, in accord.

2 *shadowed livery*: A heraldic term for a shaded or umbrated device or cognizance. Since 'umbrated' means 'drawn in outline', allowing the true colour of the 'field' to show through, Morocco implies that his dark skin is mere outline or superficial appearance, allowing the true colour of his blood to show through.

7 *reddest*: A sign of martial valour and dignity. Furness cites the Old English custom of colours for palls or hearse-cloths: 'The red of valiancy . . . kings, lords, knights and valiant soldiers: white over clergymen, in token of their profession and honest life, and over virgins and matrons.'

8 *aspect*: Look, visage (accented on the second syllable).

9 *feared*: Frightened.

13 *In terms of*: In way of.

14 *nice direction*: Scrupulous guidance.

17 *scanted*: Limited.

18 *wit*: Wisdom.

20 *fair*: An allusion to the early play on the colours, tawny, white and red.

25 *Sophy*: Emperor of Persia.

26 *Sultan Solyman*: In 1535 the Sultan Suleiman conducted an unsuccessful campaign against Persia. The two lines would seem to indicate that Morocco was one of Suleiman's commanders.

27 *o'erstare*: Outstare (the reading of Q2). Cf. *overpeer* in I.1.12.

29 *she-bear*: The bear in Shakespeare is among the most cruel aspects of nature. See *King Lear*, III.4.10–11: 'if thy flight lay toward the roaring sea | Thou'dst meet the bear i'the mouth', and *The Winter's Tale*, III.3, where sea and bear vie in cruelty.

32 *Lichas*: An attendant on Hercules (Alcides); hence the emendation of Q and F *rage* at 35 to *page*. Lansdowne alters the passage, assigning it to Bassanio: 'So were a Gyant worsted by a Dwarf.'
   dice: This game of chance focuses the wordplay throughout this scene on the hazard of the casket choice: *lott'ry*, *destiny*, *blind Fortune*, *chance*, *hazard*, *Good fortune*.

II.2

0 *Launcelot Gobbo*: Shakespeare seems to have intended a family of comic humpbacks, from the Italian '*gobba*', a hump, and '*gobbo*', hunchbacked. Jacques Callot (1592–1635) engraved two series of *commedia dell'arte* types, the *Balli di Sfessania* and the *Gobbi* or hunchbacks.

1–2 *conscience . . . fiend*: Launcelot participates in a dramatic morality, the medieval tradition of quasi-dramatic dialogue on a moral theme.

9 *Fia*: A form of 'via' – away!

15–16 *smack . . . grow to . . . taste*: A flavour (of lechery). To *grow to* was applied to burnt milk sticking to a pan.

24 *incarnation*: Q2 reads *incarnall*. Cf. Mistress Quickly's malapropism in *Henry V*, II.3.31–2: 'carnation . . . a colour he never liked'. 'Carnation colours' in miniature paintings were the flesh tones.

28 *Old Gobbo*: See first note to this scene.

32–3 *sand-blind, high-gravel-blind*: As opposed to stone-blind or totally blind.

33 *try confusions*: A malapropism for *try conclusions* (which is the reading of Q2).

40 *sonties*: Saints (from Old French or the Scottish 'zauntie').

43 *Master*: A term of some dignity applied to the rank of esquire, or to an employer as opposed to a servant.

48 *well to live*: Comfortable, well to do. This expands in a punning form, a comment on *poor* in the previous line.

52 *ergo*: Therefore.

57–8 *Sisters Three*: The Fates.

86 *what a beard*: This depends on the traditional stage business of Launcelot's kneeling for blessing with his back to Old Gobbo. It is possible that this 'recognition' by his hairiness at the point of receiving a blessing picks up ironically Shylock's earlier reference to Jacob's trick, where Jacob, the 'smooth man', is mistaken for Esau by assuming the hairy skin of kids (see note to I.3.68–71).

88 *fill-horse*: A draught-horse in the 'fills' or shafts.

96 *set up my rest*: Made up my mind.

111 *Gramercy*: God reward you greatly (Old French, '*grant merci*').

115 *infection*: Malapropism for 'affection', i.e. inclination.

120 *cater-cousins*: Perhaps from 'cater', to provide for; that is, a dependant but no blood-relation.

123 *frutify*: For 'certify'.

126 *impertinent*: For 'pertinent'.

132 *defect*: For 'effect', import.

134 *Shylock thy master spoke with me*: This is a strange incident in the relationship between Bassanio and Shylock.

135 *preferred*: Preferment, in the sense of advancement, is now most frequently used of clerical advancement.

138–40 *The old proverb is very well parted . . .*: Launcelot parts or divides the proverb between his old and new master: 'The grace of God is gear enough', that is, Bassanio has the *grace of God* and Shylock has *enough* – a competency in wealth.

144 *guarded*: Guards are the frogs or braids on a uniform or livery. Bassanio on his borrowings is fitting out a rich retinue (*rare new liveries*, 101), but Launcelot's coat is to be more heavily braided than the others. There is perhaps a suggestion of a fool's 'motley coat guarded with yellow' (*Henry VIII*, Prologue, 16).

147 *table*: The palm of the hand between the 'line of fortune' and the 'natural line'.

149 *line of life*: The circular line at the base of the thumb.

154 *gear*: Business.

155–6 *twinkling*: Q2 extends to *twinkling of an eye*.

158 *bestowed*: Stowed in the hold (of the ship bound for Belmont).

165 *suit to*: A boon to beg of (but see note to 177).

172 *liberal*: Gratiano's qualities (*Parts*) are too licentious for the delicate embassy of Bassanio.

175 *misconstered*: Misconstrued.

177 *sober habit*: The theme of outward appearance is advanced in this scene by the play on garments and liveries. Gratiano's *suit* (wish) is punningly extended on an ironic parallel to Launcelot. Later in the speech he will *look demurely*, use *observance of civility* and study a *sad ostent* (an outward show of gravity). To all this Bassanio responds at 188 that he should rather, for the moment, *put on | Your boldest suit of mirth*, completing the play on *suit*.

II.3

0 *Jessica*: It seems difficult to associate Jessica with the Iscah or Iischa of Genesis 11:29. If her name is so derived, it may also, from a Hebrew root, carry implications of treachery or spying.

10 *exhibit*: Perhaps another malapropism for 'inhibit', or, with unwonted literacy, 'my tears demonstrate what my tongue would say'.

II.4

1 *supper-time*: There is to be a masque at the meal,

like the Masque of the Senses at Timon's supper (*Timon of Athens*, Act I).

2 *Disguise*: They will be either 'visored' with small masks, or dressed in character.

5 *spoke us yet*: Bespoken or given orders for. F4 amends to *spoke as yet*.

torchbearers: A regular feature of masques.

6 *quaintly*: Curiously or elegantly.

10 *An*: If.

break up: Open (the seal).

34 *gentle*: A pun on 'Gentile' as contrast to the *faithless Jew*, her father (37).

II.5

0 *Launcelot, his man that was, the Clown*: There is possibly a suggestion here that Launcelot has ceased to be a 'natural' and become a professional clown, donning the motley.

17–18 *There is some ill a-brewing towards my rest . . .*: Dreams were ambiguous, sometimes revealing direct truth, sometimes by contraries.

20 *reproach*: For 'approach', a 'feed' line for Shylock's sardonic reply.

24 *a-bleeding*: Perhaps ominous.

24–5 *Black Monday*: The day after Easter, equated in Launcelot's deliberate nonsense with the penitential Ash Wednesday.

29 *wry-necked fife*: The fife has no curved mouthpiece but the player is described in Barnaby Rich's *Irish Hubbub* (1616): 'a fife is a wry-necked musician, for he always looks away from his instrument.'

32 *varnished faces*: The masquers were made up with the thoroughness of Elizabethan cosmetic art described in the ironic by-play between Viola and Olivia in *Twelfth Night*, I.5.220–29. Faces were painted with 'pencils' (fine brushes) with the 'carnation' tones of red and white 'truly blent'. This staining of the skin ('in grain') merited the term 'varnish'; *Timon of Athens*, a play much concerned with deceitful appearance, has the term 'painted, like his varnished friends' (IV.2.36).

34-5 *foppery . . . sober house*: Shylock has a constant
tendency to a grave puritanism which may seem *hell*
to Jessica or the *merry devil*, Launcelot.

35 *Jacob's staff*: From Genesis 32:10: 'with my staff
came I over this Jordan, and now have I gotten two
companies.' The gravity of Shylock's *sober house* is
carried on in his reference to Jacob's staff, which
was the measure of his power when he crossed
Jordan with his little band ('that is, poor and without
all provision' in the Geneva Bible margin). To
Elizabethan ears there would be a further religious
ambiguity in Shylock's possible reference to the staff
of those who went on pilgrimage to the shrine of
St James (Jacobus) of Compostella.

41 *Jewess' eye*: Q and F have *Jewes*, F3 *Jew's* and Pope
first conjectures *Jewess'*. 'A Jew's eye' was proverbial for excessive value.

42 *Hagar's offspring*: Ishmael, the son of Hagar 'the
bond-woman' to Sarah, wife of Abraham, is described
(Genesis 16:12) as 'a wild man' (in the Geneva Bible
margin: 'Or, fierce and cruel, or, as a wild ass');
Shylock wryly identifies Launcelot both with the
rebellious Ishmael and with servile descent from
Abraham, as opposed to Isaac the free born.

44 *patch*: Fool. Sir Thomas Wilson, *Art of Rhetoric* (1585):
'Patch or Coulson . . . these two in their time were
notable fools.' But perhaps from Italian '*pazzo*', a
fool (Latin '*fatuus*').

45 *profit*: Improvement (in learning rather than in wealth).

II.6

2 *hour*: Appointed time.

5-7 *O ten times faster . . . faith unforfeited*: The doves
of Venus attend a betrothal more readily than they
assist a lasting marriage.

5 *Venus' pigeons*: The doves which drew Venus' chariot.

10 *untread*: Retrace.

14 *younger*: A younger son, precisely equivalent to the
prodigal in the same line. Rowe unnecessarily emen-
ded to *younker*, a young nobleman.

15 *scarfèd*: Under full sail or possibly 'dressed overall' (but see note to 18).

16 *strumpet wind*: Like the harlots of the prodigal parable (Luke 15).

18 *With overweathered ribs*: With starting timbers, springing apart at the joints (unlike the sound, well-jointed hull, which may be the meaning of *scarfèd* at 15).

21 *abode*: Delay.

23 *thieves*: The first dark suggestion of stealth in the elopement.

35 *exchange*: An ironic term, which refers to her disguise as a boy, her abandonment of Shylock and her theft of jewels and money, with the play's prevailing overtones of commerce.

37 *pretty*: Artful (in a pejorative sense).

41–2 *candle . . . light*: Light had frequently the sense 'flippant' or 'wanton'; see V.1.130: *a light wife doth make a heavy husband*.

43 *discovery*: A military term.

45 *garnish*: Decoration (yet again with overtones of deceitful appearance).

49 *gild*: Carry more gold. This extends the sense of 'varnish' in relation to the masquers; cf. Lady Macbeth: 'I'll gild the faces of the grooms withal, | For it must seem their guilt' (*Macbeth*, II.2.56–7).

51 *by my hood*: An oath by his masque habit, or, ironically, by a monk's hood.

a gentle and no Jew: A repetition of the pun on 'Gentile'.

II.7

1 *discover*: Reveal.

11 *contains my picture*: Cf. the statement to Bassanio (III.2.40): *I am locked in one of them*; and to Arragon (II.9.5): *I am contained*.

19 *advantages*: Increase or interest. In his rejection of *shows of dross* the noble Morocco may seem to be rejecting mercenary Venice.

30 *disabling*: Disparagement.

40 *kiss this shrine, this mortal breathing saint*: By the

conventions of courtly love, the lady is an object
of veneration, like a saint or holy object within a
reliquary.

41 *Hyrcanian*: Hyrcania was south of the Caspian and
as the breeding-ground of tigers was scarcely a
'throughfare'. Cf. the Hyrcan(ian) tigers of *Macbeth*,
III.4.100, and *Hamlet*, II.2.448.

50 *base . . . gross*: Lead is both a base metal and crude.

51–2 *rib . . . immured*: These funereal terms anticipate the
carrion Death which is Morocco's reward.

51 *cerecloth*: Waxed sheet in which the body was
embalmed before being enclosed in lead for burial.

53 *ten times undervalued*: The precise comparative valu-
ation of silver to gold.

56 *angel*: A gold coin, with the device of the archangel
Michael treading down the dragon. The association
of England with 'angels' was a regular pun from St
Augustine of Canterbury to Shakespeare.

57 *insculped*: Engraved. In Richard Robinson's version
of the *Gesta Romanorum* (1577), a possible source
for this play, a lead vessel is 'insculpt' with a posy.
Shakespeare uses the word nowhere else. It should
perhaps be pointed out that he does, however, use
'insculpture', in *Timon of Athens*, V.4.67.

61 *form*: Image. A Neoplatonic term and involved with
the suggestion of substance, reality and appearance
(see note on 11 above).

63 *carrion Death*: A skull or memento mori.

69 *Gilded tombs*: Q and F have *gilded timber*, Sonnet
101 'gilded tomb'; cf. the Geneva Bible version of
Matthew 23:27: 'for ye are like unto whited tombs,
which appear beautiful outward, but are within full
of dead men's bones'; and the Bishops' Bible: 'like
unto painted sepulchres'.

75 *farewell heat*: An inversion of the 'farewell frost'
found for example in George Wapull's *Tyde Taryeth
No Man* (1576) and John Lyly's *Mother Bombie*
(1594).

79 *complexion*: Both 'appearance' and 'temperament'.

II.8

4 *the Duke* [of Venice]: The title *Doge* has become customary in English usage and this figure is familiar to us from the many admirable portraits of Dukes of Venice.

15 *ducats . . . daughter*: Cf. *The Jew of Malta*, II.1.54: 'O girl! O gold! O beauty! O my bliss!' Note that we have only Solanio's report for this ridiculous outburst by Shylock; his grief onstage is never visible.

25 *keep his day*: Fulfil his bond. Cf. *break his day* above (I.3.160).

27 *reasoned*: Talked.

28 *the narrow seas*: The English Channel.

39 *Slubber*: Carry out carelessly, scamp. Cf. its sense of 'smear' in *Othello*, I.3.224: 'slubber the gloss of your new fortunes'.

44 *ostents*: Appearances.

II.9

1–3 *Quick . . . straight . . . presently*: A hurried immediacy to rid Belmont of Arragon.

5 *I am contained*: Cf. II.7.11 and III.2.40.

13 *marriage*: Pronounced with three syllables.

14 *Lastly*: A two-syllable line.

26 *fool*: Adjectival here.

27 *fond*: Foolish.

28 *the martlet*: A swift (which builds in insecure places).

30 *force and road*: Conjectured to translate '*in vi et via*', exposed to the attack of.

32 *jump*: Agree.

38 *cozen*: Deceive.

39 *stamp*: Seal, mark.

41 *estates, degrees, and offices*: Positions, ranks and functions.

44 *cover*: Wear their hats.

49 *new varnished*: Outward adornment (as elsewhere in this play).

51 *assume*: Claim.

61 *To offend and judge are distinct offices*: Arragon cannot be tried and be a judge in his own cause.

63 *seven times trièd*: Purified seven times by heat. Cf. the significance of quintessence, distilled five times.

66 *shadows kiss*: Kiss a portrait (the shadow or counterfeit of the original sitter).

68 *iwis*: Truly (a word to fill the line).

71 *your head*: A fool's head (where he should be the head of the household). Cf. Ephesians 5:23: 'the husband is the head of the wife . . .'

78 *wroth*: Ruth (misfortune) rather than wrath (Q and F *wroath*).

89 *sensible regreets*: Substantial greetings, i.e. gifts.

90 *commends*: Commendations.
   breath: Speech.

98 *high-day*: Holiday. Cf. John 19:31: 'for that Sabbath day was a high day'; and *The Merry Wives of Windsor*, III.2.61–2: 'he speaks holiday'.

100 *post*: Messenger.

101 *Bassanio Lord, love if thy will it be*: The reading of Q and F, to be paraphrased 'Lord Bassanio, love if you will (for Portia will respond)'. Rowe's conjectural punctuation 'Bassanio, Lord Love', addresses the Cupid of the previous line, that is, 'Cupid, may this newcomer be Bassanio.'

III.1

2 *unchecked*: Unconfirmed or uncontradicted (probably the latter).

5 *flat*: Shallows.

6 *gossip*: Godmother (but here 'Dame' as a title).

9 *knapped*: Nibbled. The verb means to cut short or break, from the Dutch, '*knappen*'. Cf. Psalms 46.9: 'he . . . knappeth the spear in sunder . . .'
   ginger: Probably 'ginger-snaps' rather than the tough root-ginger.

11 *slips*: Cuttings or scions. Cf. *The Winter's Tale*, IV.4.99–100: 'I'll not put | The dibble in earth to set one slip of them . . .'

15 *the full stop*: The *stop* or halt in the manège of a trained horse. (Solanio's tongue is running away.)

19–20 *cross my prayer*: Make the sign of the cross at the

end of a prayer (with a play on 'crossing a path').
Cf. *Hamlet*, I.1.127: 'I'll cross it, though it blast me.'

27 *fledged*: Fit to fly (Q has *fledge*).
complexion: Quality or nature.

31–2 *flesh and blood . . . carrion*: Solanio purports to mis-
understand Shylock's reference to Jessica as a reference to his own fleshly nature (carrion).

37 *red wine and Rhenish*: See note to I.2.90.

40 *match*: Bargain.

42 *smug*: 'Trim' or 'complacent'.
mart: Market (the Rialto).

49 *disgraced me*: Done me disfavour.

53 *I am a Jew*: Once again Shakespeare restores the
balance in Shylock's character, making racial dignity
a greater motive-force than commercial greed. This
has been a high point in most performances. Of
Edmund Kean's speaking these words Hazlitt says that
he was 'worth a wilderness of monkeys that have aped
humanity'.

64 *sufferance*: Patience. See the note at IV.1.198 for the
contrasts between patience and revenge.

72 *Tubal*: The scene following is destroyed if Tubal's
role is the grotesque baiting of Shylock. There is
the utmost flexibility in Shylock's tone, from the
resignation of *Why there, there, there, there!* to the
near-tragic deprivation of *I had it of Leah when I
was a bachelor*. Taken with this seriousness, despite
its grotesque moments, this scene provides the proper
context for the insight that commercial loss was a
part of the nation's curse, for *I never felt it till now*.

81 *hearsed*: Coffined. Jessica, by her marriage to a
Gentile, would be dead to her race and family, to
say nothing of her treachery and theft.

86–8 *Nor no ill luck stirring but what lights o'my shoulders,
no sighs but o'my breathing, no tears but o'my shed-
ding*: In these three lines the rhythms of the prose
intensify. At the Stratford-upon-Avon production in
1962 Peter O'Toole emphasized these rhythms by
beating his breast at every repetition of *my*. At their

formal mourning, strictly Orthodox Jews accompany
the ritualized wailing by beating the breast until tears
are shed.

111 *turquoise*: The F and Q *Turkies* reflects Elizabethan
(and later) pronunciation. The turquoise was a
natural stone for a betrothal ring (though it was
semi-precious, unlike the 'seld-seen' jewels of Barabas, the Jew of Malta), for it was said 'to reconcile
man and wife' and faded or brightened with the
wearer's health.

116 *fee me an officer*: Engage a Sheriff's officer – a catch-
pole (to make the arrest of Antonio).

119 *synagogue*: This is to prepare the *oath in heaven*
which Shylock cannot break at the trial. Again the
profoundest springs in Shylock's motivation are
touched. Victor Hugo makes the appropriate comment: 'In entering his synagogue Shylock entrusts
his hatred to the safeguard of his Faith. Henceforward
his vengeance assumes a consecrated character. His
bloodthirstiness against the Christian becomes sacer-
dotal.'

III.2

4 *but it is not love*: A half-prevarication, like her
Bassanio, as I think, so was he called (I.2.109–10).

8 *a maiden hath no tongue but thought*: Either a reference to the proverb 'Maidens should be seen and
not heard' or a parallel to Rosalind's 'Do you not
know I am a woman? When I think, I must speak'
(*As You Like It*, III.2.242–3). The ambiguities and
hesitancies throughout her speech dramatically show
her dilemma between her father's will and her love.

10 *I could teach you*: A possible preparation for the song.
See note to 62 below.

15 *o'erlooked me*: Looked at me with the evil eye (a
term from witchcraft, but here used playfully).

18–19 *these naughty times . . . and their rights*: These wicked
times cheat owners of their proper possessions.

22 *piece*: Q and F *peiʒe*, usually explained as derived
from Old French '*peser*', to retard by hanging weights;

cf. *Richard III*, V.3.106: 'Lest leaden slumber peise me down tomorrow . . .' But Rowe suggested the verb 'to piece', which better answers to *eke*, *draw out* and *stay* in the next two lines.

23 *eke*: The two words *piece* and *eke* occur in the Prologues to *Henry V*. In the Prologue to Act I: 'Piece out our imperfections' (23); and to Act III: 'eke out our performance' (35).

29 *fear*: To be apprehensive of (lest his love should not succeed).

32 *rack*: Silvayn's *Orator* (1596), from which Shakespeare may have taken hints for the bond plot, has several instances of torture on the rack which produced false confessions of guilt. Dr Lopez, Queen Elizabeth's physician and a Jew who had converted to Christianity, executed when found guilty of conspiracy with Catholics in a plot to murder the Queen, 'pleaded . . . he had much belied himself in his confession to save himself from racking'.

40 *I am locked in one of them*: Referring to Portia's portrait.

43–53 *Let music sound while he doth make his choice . . .*: This speech is one of the most elaborate analyses of stage music in Shakespeare, drawing attention to the dramatic and emotional significance of the song while Bassanio chooses. It proceeds to a formal division of the music's significance: if Bassanio fails he will have his swan-song (cf. *King John*, V.7.21–2: 'faint swan | Who chants a doleful hymn to his own death'); if successful it will be a *flourish* or fanfare at the moment of a royal crowning; throughout it will be both a lover's *aubade* or dawn-song (*in break of day*) and an *epithalamium* or marriage-song (for the *bridegroom's ear*).

55 *Alcides*: Hercules. A further reference to the choice as Herculean (cf. Morocco's choice, II.1.35). Portia speaks of Bassanio's *more love*, since Hercules rescued Hesione for a material reward, the horses which King Laomedon of Troy, her father, had promised

(Ovid, *Metamorphoses*, VII, lines 237–9: 'His daughter
. . . stout Hercules delivering safe and sound, |
Required his steeds which were the hire for which
he did compound'). The contrast of love and palpable
reward is an ironic comment on Bassanio's initial
motive, the *golden fleece*.

58 *Dardanian*: Trojan.

59 *blearèd*: Tear-blotched.

62 *A song the whilst Bassanio comments*: A much-
discussed stage direction. Portia has declared (10–11)
that she *could teach you* | *How to choose right*.
Ingenious suggestions concerning the rhymes *bred*,
head etc. with 'lead' argue that the song is a 'broad
hint'. The argument is in fact more delicate. It is
given an elaborate context (see 43–53); the song
itself is a precise account of the death of *fancy*
which is a superficial concern with outward appearance, and dies in the cradle, *the eyes*; finally, at 73,
Bassanio in the single word *So* links his meditations
on the three caskets with the argument of the song.
This is an altogether subtler texture of meaning than
a mere hint from Portia to Bassanio, which would
belittle both their relationship and her good faith.

75 *In law*: It is characteristic of the tenor of the play
that Bassanio's first example should be legal.
tainted: Evil-tasting, like stale meat, which must be
seasoned (76) by spices to make it palatable. Cf. *Much
Ado About Nothing*, IV.1.140–41: 'salt too little which
may season give | To her foul tainted flesh'.

81 *simple*: Palpable, uncomplicated.

83–4 *false* | *As stairs of sand*: Probably 'as treacherous as
steps cut in a sand-hill'; 'bulwarks of sand', echoing
the Q and F spelling *stayers*, in the sense of 'prop,
support or stay' is also suggested.

86 *livers white as milk*: Cf. *Henry IV, Part II*, IV.3.102–4:
'blood . . . cold and settled, left the liver white and
pale, which is the badge of pusillanimity and coward-
ice'.

87 *excrement*: Outward growth, excrescence.

89 *purchased by the weight*: In the form of cosmetics.

92 *crispèd snaky golden locks*: Courtesans were regularly painted by the Venetian painters of the Renaissance with crimped gold hair; see Carpaccio's *The Courtesans* in the Museo Correr, Venice.

96 *sepulchre*: Cf. Sonnet 68, a description of 'beauty's dead fleece':

> Before the golden tresses of the dead,
> The right of sepulchers, were shorn away
> To live a second life on second head . . .

97 *guilèd*: Treacherous. F2 reads *guilded*.

99 *Indian beauty*: Dark beauty (as opposed to the Elizabethan ideal).

103 *drudge*: Mere servant of exchange and commerce.

108–14 *How all the other passions . . . I surfeit*: Portia's response is given both intensity and aesthetic control by being bounded within three rhymed couplets.

112 *rain*: Either 'weep tears of joy in moderation' or, if the *raine* of Q and F and the *reine* of Q3 indicate the modern English 'rein', as Dr Johnson conjectured, then it is a term from the manège of horses and implies, 'Do not allow your joy to run away with you.'

excess: A term of usury which punningly extends the mercantile theme into that of personal relations; 'the rent that's due to love'.

115 *counterfeit*: Portrait. There was a constant ambiguity in the Elizabethan aesthetic of portraiture. Likeness was prized but it was also (as *Timon of Athens* demonstrates in the conflict between the Poet and the Painter) regarded as a 'conceit deceitful' (*The Rape of Lucrece*, l.1423). The ambiguous undertone in *counterfeit* hints at the prevailing concern that appearance shall match reality; cf. these phrases in *Timon of Athens*: 'a pretty mocking of the life' (I.1.36); 'It tutors nature . . . livelier than life' (38–9), 'The painting is almost the natural man' (161), 'Thou drawest a counterfeit | Best in all Athens' (V.1.79–80).

127–8 *substance . . . shadow*: The concern for reality behind
       the superficial is in these words given a Neoplatonic
       expression.

131 *choose not by the view*: The argument is here locked up.
      Unlike those who have chosen by external appearance,
      Bassanio chooses by quality and not by mere sight.

140 *by note*: By a bill of dues (a commercial term). With
      affectionate irony Bassanio, like Portia at 112, trans-
      ports terms of commerce into love.

148 *confirmed, signed, ratified*: Further legal-commercial
      terms. This by-play, half jest, half earnest, uniting
      the two main aspects of the play, is extended in the
      mathematical terms of Portia's next speech, 153–8:
      trebled twenty times, your account, sum, in gross, with
      the significant interpolation: *virtues, beauties, livings,
      friends*, where *livings* implies possessions, tenures (as
      in the ecclesiastical sense).

153–5 *I would be trebled twenty times myself . . .*: The reading
        here follows the lineation in Q1, the third line being
        an alexandrine. Some editors realign to place the
        alexandrine one line earlier:

          I would be trebled twenty times myself,
          A thousand times more fair, ten thousand times more
            rich,
          That only to stand high in your account . . .

        The extra syllables weaken the powerful duplication
        of number at 154, *A thousand times . . . ten thou-
        sand times*. The Q reading gives the actor a char-
        acteristic run-on between 154 and 155, and the pause
        after *more rich* retains the feeling of a blank-verse
        line in the words that follow.

158 *sum of something*: The Q reading; F has *sum of
      nothing*. In either reading it is a diffident setting aside
      of her wealth and a concentration on her youth,
      with the determination (like Katherine the Shrew)
      to take her husband as her lord.

167 *converted*: A final momentary return to the commer-

cial; the converting of funds from one owner to
another.

171–3   *ring . . . ruin of your love*: In the serio-comic tone
of the scene, the ring could have a significance
similar to that of Othello's handkerchief. It is deli-
cately related to the potential tragedy of Antonio's
trial and finally turned aside in the closing speech
of the play in an inoffensive indecency.

181–2   *something . . . nothing*: A playful echo of Portia's
sum of something.

198   *mistress . . . maid*: It is important to estimate the
social distinction with nicety: Nerissa, like Maria in
Twelfth Night, is a 'waiting-gentlewoman', no common servant, and therefore wholly worthy to marry
a gentleman.

199–200   *intermission | No more pertains to me, my lord, than
you*: I, my lord, have no more escaped than you (a
mock-rueful jest).

215   *stake down*: Nerissa means 'a wager'; Gratiano
(216–17) takes it in the bawdy sense 'with a limp
penis'.

218   *infidel*: This return to Jessica is a reminder of the
religious undertone conveyed in *misbeliever . . . infidel
. . . Jew . . . become a Christian*.

221   *my new interest here*: Bassanio's language cannot
remain long divorced from the commercial.

223   *very*: Veritable, true.

236   *estate*: Both 'condition' and 'fortune'.

237   *stranger*: Alien (a further emphasis on Jessica's status).

239   *royal merchant*: A merchant prince. In Elizabeth's day
Gresham, the most notable merchant-banker of the
age, was given this title.

241   *We are the Jasons, we have won the Fleece*: With a
punning return to the unabashed self-aggrandize-
ment with which Bassanio first set out on his Belmont
venture, he prepares the irony of the pun *fleece*—
'fleets' between this line and the next.

243   *shrewd*: Evil, misfortunate. Cf. beshrew, beshrow,
used playfully throughout.

246–7 *the constitution | Of any constant man*: The temper
       of a man whose blood and judgement were well
       mingled.

262 *mere*: Sheer, absolute. Cf. Queen Elizabeth's boast
     to her people that she was 'mere English'.

267 *hit*: Hit the mark, an echo of Bassanio's archery
     analogy in the first scene.

278 *impeach the freedom of the state*: Imperil the freedom
     and equity of Venetian law.

280 *magnificoes*: The Venetian rulers under the Doge.

282 *envious*: Malicious.

285 *countrymen*: Jessica's reference to two members of
     her father's race and her own as his *countrymen* has
     an alien sound. Shylock's term is *tribe*.

295 *ancient Roman honour*: 'Antique Roman', 'high Roman
     fashion' – the type of stoical dignity and honour,
     and a term of commendation for Dane, Egyptian
     or Venetian.

303 *church*: The vow in II.1 is taken in *the temple* (44);
     the sacrament of marriage here in *church*.

312 *cheer*: Appearance, countenance.

III.3

This short scene has a passionate intensity. The character of Shylock, implacable now, with religious
sanctions (*I have sworn an oath*, 5) matures towards
its greatest complexity.

9 *naughty*: Wicked.
   fond: Foolish.

20 *bootless*: Hopeless, unavailing.

22 *forfeitures*: Process of debt when a bond became forfeit.

26 *deny*: Prevent.

27 *commodity*: Traffic, commercial relations (on the ease
    and propriety of which the wealth of Venice
    depended).

32 *bated*: Reduced. Cf. 'bated breath'.

III.4

0 *Balthasar*: The verse appears to demand the pronunciation Balthasár (or Bálthasar).

2 *conceit*: Conception.

3 *godlike amity*: Lorenzo refers to a discussion in full flight between himself and Portia. She has admitted, despite the depth of her love for Bassanio, the profound claim of platonic love or friendship between Bassanio and Antonio.

9 *customary bounty*: 'Your accustomed goodness' ('*bonté*') or 'the acts of kindness demanded by the custom or manners of gentility'.

12 *waste*: Spend.

13 *equal*: Q and F *egall*, from French '*égal*', i.e. matched, equivalent.

15 *lineaments*: 'Features' or, more probably, 'temperamental qualities'.

20 *semblance*: Image, exact correspondence of. Cf. 'semblable' in *Timon of Athens*, IV.3.22: 'His semblable, yea himself, Timon disdains.'

25 *husbandry and manage*: Stewardship and management. 'To husband' is still used in a frugal sense; see *Macbeth*, II.1.4–5: 'There's husbandry in heaven: | Their candles are all out.'

31 *monastery*: There was in fact a Benedictine Convent near the river Brenta on the road between Padua and Venice; in this area the magnificoes of Venice had many country residences.

49 *Padua*: Q and F read *Mantua*, an error, since it disagrees with IV.1.109 and V.1.268, and Padua was the centre of Civil Law studies in Italy.

51 *look what*: Whatever.

52 *imagined*: All imaginable.

53 *traject*: Q and F read *tranect*, probably a compositor's misreading of a manuscript 'traiect', probably from Italian '*traghetto*', a ferry, found in John Florio's *World of Words* (1598); and Thomas Coryat notes the 'thirteen ferries or passages [in Venice] which they commonly call Traghetti'. Twenty miles from Padua, on the Brenta, there is a dam to control the waters short of the Venetian marshes; this may have constituted a ferry, or bridge, known to Shakespeare by travellers' hearsay.

61 *accomplishèd*: Equipped.

69 *quaint*: Ingenious.

72 *I could not do withal*: I could not help it.

77 *Jacks*: Contemptible fellows.

78 *Why, shall we turn to men*: Nerissa's question means, of course, 'Shall we become men?' Portia, jokingly, takes it in a sexual sense: 'Shall we offer our arses to men?'

III.5

1 *sins of the father*: A constant theme of Jewish theological history: 'The fathers have eaten a sour grape and the children's teeth are set on edge'; see the note below at IV.1.203.

3 *fear you*: Fear for you.

4 *agitation*: For cogitation?

4–5 *be o'good cheer*: Very near blasphemy, in quoting the claim of salvation in a sentence of damnation: 'be of good cheer, I have overcome the world' (John 16:33).

14–15 *Scylla . . . Charybdis*: The cave of Scylla and the whirlpool of Charybdis, the Straits of Messina.

17 *saved by my husband*: Cf. Paul, 1 Corinthians 7:14: 'the unbelieving wife is sanctified by the husband.'

20 *enow*: Enough.

29 *are out*: Have quarrelled.

49–50 *cover . . . duty*: A play on covered dishes in preparation for dinner and the head covered as a sign of rank.

58 *humours and conceits*: Literally 'inclinations and thoughts', but punningly for 'wit'. The puns of this scene, lightly stressing the themes with which Jessica is involved, prepare for the gravity of the trial.

60–64 *suited . . . Garnished*: A play on the fool's motley. It has been interpreted as a compliment to Will Kempe, who probably played Launcelot.

65 *Defy the matter*: Refuse to make sense (refuse to elucidate the matter).

How cheer'st thou: How art thou?

77 *Pawned*: Staked, added.

IV.I

0   *Enter the Duke, the magnificoes*: The constitution and
    status of this court is ambiguous. In the course of
    the scene the law mutates from a Civil to a Criminal
    cause. In the former case, Venice had a court of
    forty judges, for the latter a similar composition but
    – until the fourteenth century – presided over by
    the Doge. It is clear that even if he knew the
    Venetian law, Shakespeare was not concerned with
    'realism'.

4   *stony adversary*: The scene opens with blatant
    partiality.

7   *qualify*: Moderate.

13 *tyranny*: Violence (whether of emotion or of power
    over a subject).

20–21 *strange . . . strange*: Unusual . . . unnatural.

21 *apparent*: Clear, manifest.

26 *moiety*: Portion (not necessarily a half, as '*moitié*').

32 *Turks . . . Tartars*: Again similar in import to the
    categories of 'Jews, Turks, Infidels, and Heretics' in
    the Good Friday Collect; see note to 1.3.108.

34 *gentle answer, Jew*: The climax of the punning on
    'Gentile'.

36 *holy Sabbath*: Shylock responds in kind to the Gentile
    plea.

43 *my humour*: My whim (or possibly a pun in the sense
    of 'witty caprice' and the fixed constitution of the
    Jonsonian 'humour').

46 *baned*: Poisoned.

47 *gaping*: Prepared for table, with fruit in its mouth.

49 *sings i'th'nose*: The bagpipe's drone, perhaps like the
    whining, nasal voice of the Puritan.

50–51 *affection . . . passion*: Cf. III.1.53–5: *Hath not a Jew . . .
    senses, affections, passions?*; *affections* are 'desires',
    related to the will; *passions* are the emotions associated
    with the *affections*; hence here *Master of passion*.

55 *necessary cat*: The cat is a domestic necessity to keep
    down mice (this, with the adjective *harmless* to distin-
    guish it from a cat which is a witch's familiar).

56 *woollen*: Covered with woollen cloth.

60 *lodged*: Deep-seated.

    certain: Fixed.

62 *A losing suit*: A suit involving inevitable material loss for Shylock. A moment of irony for the audience, anticipating the *peripeteia* later in the scene by which Shylock is condemned to lose all.

70 *question*: Argue (a term of formal disputation).

76 *high-tops*: Cf. the mast of I.1.28.

77 *fretten*: Fretted.

88–9 *mercy . . . judgement*: A further anticipation of Shylock's reversal of fortune, and of the references to the Lord's Prayer in IV.1.198.

90–100 *You have among you many a purchased slave . . .*: This is the most intense expression of Shylock's desired power over Antonio; the *pound of flesh* is the purchased life and Antonio a slave dearly bought to Shylock's will.

114–15 *tainted wether of the flock,* | *Meetest for death*: An interesting Gentile statement; in Jewish law a sacrificial beast had to be wholly unblemished.

114 *wether*: Ram.

123 *sole . . . soul*: There is a parallel to this pun in *Romeo and Juliet*, I.4.14–15: 'You have dancing shoes | With nimble soles. I have a soul of lead' – but there is a still graver undertone in Gratiano's speech, anticipating Shylock's damnation.

125 *hangman's axe*: Cf. *Measure for Measure*, IV.2.46–9: 'your hangman . . . your block and your axe'.

128 *inexecrable*: The reading *inexecrable* is found in the Qs and F1 and it was amended to *inexorable* in F3. *inexecrable* is an attractive reading ('cannot be sufficiently execrated') and it is paralleled by the line in *Faustus* 'thou damned witch and execrable dog'. While this parallel appears to make the Q reading certain, *inexorable* has also much to be said for it. The context relates to prayer ('can no prayers pierce thee?') and *inexorable* may be read 'cannot be moved by prayer', from '*orare*', to pray.

129 *And for thy life let justice be accused*: And because
of your very existence, let justice itself be brought
into question.

131 *Pythagoras*: He propounded the doctrine of the 'trans-
migration of souls'. Cf. *Twelfth Night*, IV.2.49–50.

133–4 *currish . . . wolf*: This is argued as a reference to
the execution of Dr Lopez ('*lupus*' – wolf).

167 *take your place*: Portia's status (like her precise location within the court) is ambiguous: is she a consultant
to give 'counsel's opinion'; advocate for Antonio; or
judge? If the last, her place, at the Duke's invitation, would be on the bench.

171 *Which is the merchant here? And which the Jew*: The
relative dramatic significance of Antonio and Shylock
has fluctuated in the published and stage history of
the play. Lansdowne's adaptation is *The Jew of Venice*
and by the nineteenth century Shylock was of such
central significance that at his defeat at the end of
this act the play was frequently brought to a close.

177 *within his danger*: In his power. A legal term expressed
in the 'law French' '*estre en son danger*'; Old French
'*dangier*', absolute power. The word could also signify
'debt'.

198 *that same prayer*: The Lord's Prayer: 'forgive us our
trespasses' or (in the Bishops' Bible) 'forgive us our
debts as we forgive our debtors'. Note also the
marginal note in the Geneva Bible, Matthew 6:12,
of significance to the theme of *The Merchant of
Venice*: 'They that forgive wrongs, to them sins are
forgiven, but revenge is prepared for them that
revenge' (see III.1.62–5, Shylock on Christian
revenge).

200 *mitigate*: Moderate. But *mercy* is part of the customary
'plea in mitigation' *after* guilt has been pronounced.

203 *My deeds upon my head*: If this reference be to the
trial of Christ (Matthew 27:25: 'His blood be on us
and on our children'), Shylock has made its significance sharper, taking the guilt solely to himself.
Unlike Launcelot in his reference to inherited guilt

in III.5.1–2 (see note above), Shylock extends the
pattern of references by assimilating the cry at
Christ's trial ('on *us* and on our children') to the
teaching of Jeremiah 31 ('Then shall it no more be
said. The fathers have eaten a sour grape and the
children's teeth are set on edge, for every one shall
die for his own misdeeds' (29–30)); Shylock here
assumes full personal responsibility for his pursuit
of Antonio's life.

215–16 *no power in Venice | Can alter a decree establishèd*: Laws
in Venice had the immutability attributed to those
of the Medes and Persians. See *Il Pecorone*: 'Venice
was a place where the law was enforced, and the
Jew had his rights fully and publicly.'

220 *Daniel*: Daniel was the young judge in the story of
Susannah and the Elders; he also detected the false
priest of Bel in Bel and the Dragon (both from the
Apocrypha); see Ezekiel 28:3: 'Behold, thou thinkest
thyself wiser than Daniel.' One might have expected
Shylock to have cited Solomon as the type of wise
judge and Lansdowne's version extends the reference: 'A *Daniel*, a *David*: So ripe in Wisdom And
so young in years! A second *Solomon*.' But Portia's
'youth' more accords with Daniel than with Solomon.

225 *an oath in heaven*: Taken with Tubal at the synagogue.

252 *balance*: Known in Shakespeare's day in this plural
form.

271–8 *Tell her the process of Antonio's end . . .*: A 'witty'
speech throughout: *process* puns on 'manner' and
'legal process'; Portia is in fact his *judge* and an
auditor of his speech; 'all his heart' is precisely the
penalty sought by Shylock. This witty nonchalance
(the quality of *sprezzatura* cultivated by the courtier)
was especially to be shown at point of death.
Lansdowne, in a later, less witty age, amplifies the
pun to extinction: 'for I would have my Heart Seen
by my Friend'.

293 *Barabbas*: He who 'for insurrection' was condemned

to death and was released as an act of clemency at
the Passover in place of Christ. The close association of the people's cry for Barabbas at the same
time that they willed that Christ's blood be 'on us,
and on our children' adds an ironic depth to this
line in Shylock's mouth.

302 *Tarry a little*: Shakespeare dramatically points, with
this verbal gesture, the precise moment of *peripeteia*.

326–7 *twentieth part | Of one poor scruple*: One grain by weight.

331 *on the hip*: See note to I.3.43.

346–54 *If it be proved against an alien* . . .: These are the
conditions which the Duke's mercy and Antonio's
modify; see the note to IV.1.378.

373 *You take my life*: Cf. Ecclesiasticus 34.22: 'Who so
robbeth his neighbour of his living, doth as great
sin as though he slew him to death.'

378 *quit the fine for*: It would seem that Shylock is treated
with total clemency: his life is saved, Antonio holds
one half of his property *in trust* for Jessica; and this
ambiguous sentence must imply 'to quit (i.e. remit,
settle – from '*quietus*') the fine imposed of half his
goods'. This was Lansdowne's reading: 'To quit the
fine of one half of his goods.' Shylock therefore
suffers no physical penalties – and in Lansdowne's
play his enforced Christianity is omitted.

380 *in use*: A legal term, the device of 'a conveyance to
user', whereby an estate intended for inheritance by
a second person (Jessica in this instance) is made
over to a third person (Antonio) for security of
inheritance. In full legal terms, Antonio would be
declared seised of half Shylock's estate to the use
of Lorenzo and Jessica after Shylock's death.

384 *presently*: Forthwith.
become a Christian: Thomas Coryat declares of the
Jews of Venice that 'all their goods are confiscated
as soon as they embrace Christianity . . . and so
disclog their souls and consciences'. Shakespeare
clearly excludes such an action and quotes the relevant scriptural text (373 above).

395 *godfathers*: A canting term for a jury.

401 *presently*: Without delay.

403 *gratify*: Be courteous to, reward.

409 *cope*: Give in recompense (? from Old English '*ceapan*', to buy and sell, as in cheapen, Cheapside, Chipping Camden and chapman).

448 *commandèment*: A quadrisyllable here, though usually a trisyllable elsewhere in Shakespeare, except in *Henry VI, Part I*, I.3.20: 'From him I have express commandement . . .'

452 *presently*: At once.

IV.2

15 *old swearing*: Ample oaths (a colloquial augmentative, paralleled by the Italian '*vecchio*' in the same sense; cf. 'a high old time').

V.1

It has been customary to speak of the gracious lyricism of this opening to the fifth act, a contrast to the sombre trial scene. In fact Shakespeare rarely indulges in such simple contrasts. This is no more an unflawed lyricism than the close of *A Midsummer Night's Dream* or the ironic opening of *Twelfth Night*. This playfulness of the lovers has sombre undertones in the literary parallels which they cite in their mock encounter: Troilus, Cressida, Thisbe, Dido and Medea. This is then a 'flyting match', mocking the traditional devotees of love, such as those described in Chaucer's *Legend of Good Women*, the *Parliament of Fowls* and the *Knight's Tale*. These devotees of Venus were often illustrated in later medieval tapestries and manuscripts.

The first fourteen lines of the scene are indebted both to Chaucer and to Ovid's *Metamorphoses*, probably (as elsewhere in the play) in Golding's translation.

4–6 *Troilus . . .* | *Where Cressid lay*: Cf. Chaucer, *Troilus and Criseyde*, V, 647–67.

7 *Thisbe*: Cf. *A Midsummer Night's Dream*, Act V, and Chaucer, *Legend of Good Women*, 796–812.

10 *Dido with a willow in her hand*: From Chaucer's

Legend of Good Women but more accurately reflecting
the details of Ariadne's story than Dido's. The willow
was a sign of forsaken love; see Desdemona's willow
song and Spenser, *Faerie Queene*, I.1.9: 'worn of
forlorn Paramours'.

13 *Medea*: Though she is associated with Thisbe and
Dido in Chaucer, the gathering of herbs at full moon
is from Ovid, *Metamorphoses*, VII; in Golding's translation, when the moon shone 'Most full of light',
Medea 'gat her out of doors and wandered up and
down'.

15–21 *steal . . . unthrift . . . Stealing her soul . . . ne'er a
true [vow] . . . shrew*: These lines continue, despite
the playfulness, the darker implications of the tragic
lovers cited.

22 *Slander*: Jessica's previous speech, questioning Lorenzo's fidelity.

24 *Stephano*: The verse appears to demand the pronunciation Stepháno.

39 *Sola, sola*: Launcelot imitates the sound of a post
horse as he gallops in.

46–7 *post . . . horn*: The post horn becomes a cornucopia
in Launcelot's pun.

53 *music*: A consort of instruments, a small orchestra.

57 *Become*: Befit.
    touches: Phrases (derived from the touching or
fingering the strings).

58 *floor of heaven*: Both the sky and the overhanging
canopy of the stage, painted with stars and heavenly signs.

59 *patens*: The dish, of silver or gold, from which the
consecrated bread of the eucharist is served.

60–63 *There's not the smallest orb . . .*: The music of the spheres
has been referred to many sources: the Pythagorean
doctrine of numbers and harmony which Wordsworth
echoes in *Ode on the Power of Sound*; Plato, *The Republic*,
X; nearer Shakespeare's day Montaigne, *On Custom*
(translated by John Florio, 1603), and, still nearer,
Richard Hooker, *Ecclesiastical Policy*, V (1597):

'Touching musical harmony . . . such is the force there-
of . . . that some have been thereby induced to think
that the soul itself by nature is or hath in it harmony.'
There may be also a scriptural echo of Job 38:7: 'Where
wast thou when the morning stars sang together?'

64 *muddy vesture*: The contrast between the soul and
its 'muddy vesture' the body was a Neoplatonic
doctrine familiar to Shakespeare and may be echoed
in Hamlet's longing for the dissolution of 'this too
too sullied [or solid] flesh' (I.2.12). Italian Neoplaton-
ism (which Shakespeare frequently echoes) carried
the implications of this doctrine still further in a
complex mythology depicting the release of the soul
from the body's bondage. This could be depicted in
religious form, for example in the flaying of St
Bartholomew, in Michelangelo's *Last Judgement* in
the Sistine Chapel; or in secular form in the flaying
of Marsyas by Apollo. (See Edgar Wind, *Pagan
Mysteries in the Renaissance* (1958).)

66 *Diana*: As moon goddess of chastity, appropriately
invoked here.

79 *the poet*: Ovid.

81 *stockish*: Blockish, brutal.

87 *Erebus*: A dark place on the way to Hades.

90–91 *candle . . . naughty world*: Cf. Matthew 5:16: 'Let
your light so shine before men that they may see
your good works . . .'

94 *A substitute shines brightly as a king*: A regular
Shakespearian situation; cf. Angelo in *Measure for
Measure* and Lorenzo as Portia's substitute in this play.

98 *your music*: Cf. 53 above.

99 *respect*: Comparison.

109 *How the moon sleeps with Endymion*: If this refers to
the two lovers, Lorenzo is identified with Endymion
and Jessica with Diana who caused him to sleep on
Latmos.

121 *tucket*: A trumpet flourish (Italian '*toccata*').

127–8 *We should hold day . . . the sun*: A puzzling speech,
perhaps rightly explained by Malone: 'If you would

always walk in the night, it would be day with us,
as it now is on the other side of the globe.'

135–8 *bound . . . acquitted*: It is characteristic of this final
act that the grave and even the potentially tragic
themes of the play are punned on lightly.

144 *Would he were gelt*: Would he were a eunuch.

148 *posy*: An inscription on the inner surface of a ring,
common in England in the seventeenth century. They
were found also from classical times on the outside.

156 *respective*: Careful. Cf. *Romeo and Juliet*, III.1.123:
'respective lenity'.

162 *scrubbèd*: Short. Warton suggested the emendation
'stubbed', since small birds were colloquially known
as 'stubbed young ones'. But two instances from
Philemon Holland's translation of Pliny's *Natural
History* confirm Shakespeare's reading: 'Such will
never prove fair trees, but shrubs only'; 'Verily a
little scrubby plant it is, or shrub rather.'

199 *virtue*: Power (Latin '*virtus*', Italian '*virtù*'). This was
a term of some ambiguity in Shakespeare's day, rarely
having moral overtones. Cf. Tamburlaine's declaration that 'virtue solely is the sum of glory' with the
gospel declaration that at the performance of a
miracle Christ knew that 'virtue had gone out of him'.
In the present passage, though the tone and the
bantering echo of Bassanio's rhythms in Portia's
reply keep the tension light, the *virtue* of the ring
reminds the playgoer of Shakespeare's later gravity
over Desdemona's kerchief.

206 *ceremony*: A sacred symbol.

210 *civil doctor*: A pun on 'Doctor of Civil Law' and 'a
courteous doctor'.

230 *Argus*: The hundred-eyed.

237, 307 *clerk's pen . . . Nerissa's ring*: These two bawdy puns
on the male and female sexual genitalia, both referred
to Nerissa, maintain the prevailing tone of this act,
poised between romantic comedy and high seriousness.

244 *doubly sees himself*: A further light handling of the

centrally serious theme of deceitful appearance; as
applied by Portia to Bassanio it picks up lightly the
motive of the casket scene.

251–2 *bound . . . soul . . . forfeit*: Antonio enters the witty
exchange. The references to *bond* and *forfeit* are
deepened by the middle term, *soul*, for in the former
bond Antonio wagered no more than his flesh.

266 *grossly*: Licentiously.

294 *manna*: The word comes appropriately (food in a
desert place) after Nerissa's reference to *Jessica* and
rich Jew. Shakespeare probably borrowed a pun here
from the marginal glosses in the Geneva and Bishops'
Bibles, which rounds off the Jewish element in the
play. For in Exodus 16:15 ('they said every one to
his neighbour, It is Manna') both Bibles refer in the
margin to Manna (or 'Man') in the same terms:
'which signifieth a part, portion or gift'.

298 *upon inter'gatories*: It is characteristic that Portia's
final speech should be in legal terms, a reference to
the questioning of witnesses on oath.

The National: three theatres and so much more...

www.nationaltheatre.org.uk

In its three theatres on London's South Bank, the National presents an eclectic mix of new plays and classics, with seven or eight shows in repertory at any one time.

And there's more. Step inside and enjoy free exhibitions, backstage tours, talks and readings, a great theatre bookshop and plenty of places to eat and drink.

Sign-up as an e-member at www.nationaltheatre.org.uk/join and we'll keep you up-to-date with everything that's going on.

NT NATIONAL THEATRE
SOUTH BANK
LONDON SE1 9PX

PENGUIN SHAKESPEARE

ALL'S WELL THAT ENDS WELL
WILLIAM SHAKESPEARE

WWW.PENGUINSHAKESPEARE.COM

A poor physician's daughter cures the King of France, and in return is promised the hand of any nobleman she wishes. But the man she chooses, the proud young Count of Rosillion, refuses to consummate the forced marriage and flees to Florence. Depicting the triumph of trickery over youthful arrogance, *All's Well that Ends Well* is among Shakespeare's darkest romantic comedies, yet it remains a powerful tribute to the strength of love.

This book includes a general introduction to Shakespeare's life and the Elizabethan theatre, a separate introduction to *All's Well That Ends Well*, a chronology of his works, suggestions for further reading, an essay discussing performance options on both stage and screen, and a commentary.

Edited by Barbara Everett

With an introduction by Janette Dillon

General Editor: Stanley Wells

PENGUIN SHAKESPEARE

AS YOU LIKE IT
WILLIAM SHAKESPEARE

WWW.PENGUINSHAKESPEARE.COM

When Rosalind is banished by her uncle, who has usurped her father's throne, she flees to the Forest of Arden where her exiled father holds court. There, dressed as a boy to avoid discovery, she encounters the man she loves – now a fellow exile – and resolves to remain in disguise to test his feelings for her. A gloriously sunny comedy, *As You Like It* is an exuberant combination of concealed identities and verbal jousting, reconciliations and multiple weddings.

This book includes a general introduction to Shakespeare's life and the Elizabethan theatre, a separate introduction to *As You Like It*, a chronology of his works, suggestions for further reading, an essay discussing performance options on both stage and screen, and a commentary.

Edited by H. J. Oliver

With an introduction by Katherine Duncan-Jones

General Editor: Stanley Wells

PENGUIN SHAKESPEARE

CYMBELINE
WILLIAM SHAKESPEARE

WWW.PENGUINSHAKESPEARE.COM

The King of Britain, enraged by his daughter's disobedience in marrying against his wishes, banishes his new son-in-law. Having fled to Rome, the exiled husband makes a foolish wager with a villain he encounters there – gambling on the fidelity of his abandoned wife. Combining courtly menace and horror, comedy and melodrama, *Cymbeline* is a moving depiction of two young lovers driven apart by deceit and self-doubt.

This book includes a general introduction to Shakespeare's life and the Elizabethan theatre, a separate introduction to *Cymbeline*, a chronology of his works, suggestions for further reading, an essay discussing performance options on both stage and screen, and a commentary.

Edited with an introduction by John Pitcher

General Editor: Stanley Wells

PENGUIN SHAKESPEARE

MEASURE FOR MEASURE
WILLIAM SHAKESPEARE

WWW.PENGUINSHAKESPEARE.COM

In the Duke's absence from Vienna, his strict deputy Angelo revives an ancient law forbidding sex outside marriage. The young Claudio, whose fiancée is pregnant, is condemned to death by the law. His sister Isabella, soon to become a nun, pleads with Lord Angelo for her brother's life. But her purity so excites Angelo that he offers her a monstrous bargain – he will save Claudio if Isabella will visit him that night.

This book includes a general introduction to Shakespeare's life and the Elizabethan theatre, a separate introduction to *Measure for Measure*, a chronology of his works, suggestions for further reading, an essay discussing performance options on both stage and screen by Nicholas Arnold, and a commentary.

Edited by J. M. Nosworthy

With an introduction by Julia Briggs

General Editor: Stanley Wells

Penguin Shakespeare

A MIDSUMMER NIGHT'S DREAM
WILLIAM SHAKESPEARE

WWW.PENGUINSHAKESPEARE.COM

A young woman flees Athens with her lover, only to be pursued by her would-be husband and by her best friend. Unwittingly, all four find themselves in an enchanted forest where fairies and sprites soon take an interest in human affairs, dispensing magical love potions and casting mischievous spells. In this dazzling comedy, confusion ends in harmony, as love is transformed, misplaced, and – ultimately – restored.

This book includes a general introduction to Shakespeare's life and the Elizabethan theatre, a separate introduction to *A Midsummer Night's Dream*, a chronology of his works, suggestions for further reading, an essay discussing performance options on both stage and screen, and a commentary.

Edited by Stanley Wells

With an introduction by Helen Hackett

General Editor: Stanley Wells

PENGUIN SHAKESPEARE

ROMEO AND JULIET
WILLIAM SHAKESPEARE

WWW.PENGUINSHAKESPEARE.COM

A young man and woman meet by chance and fall instantly in love. But their families are bitter enemies, and in order to be together the two lovers must be prepared to risk everything. Set in a city torn apart by feuds and gang warfare, *Romeo and Juliet* is a dazzling combination of passion and hatred, bawdy comedy and high tragedy.

This book includes a general introduction to Shakespeare's life and the Elizabethan theatre, a separate introduction to *Romeo and Juliet*, a chronology of his works, suggestions for further reading, an essay discussing performance options on both stage and screen, and a commentary.

Edited by T. J. B. Spencer

With an introduction by Adrian Poole

General Editor: Stanley Wells

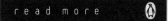
PENGUIN SHAKESPEARE

THE TWO GENTLEMEN OF VERONA
WILLIAM SHAKESPEARE

WWW.PENGUINSHAKESPEARE.COM

Leaving behind both home and beloved, a young man travels to Milan to meet his closest friend. Once there, however, he falls in love with his friend's new sweetheart and resolves to seduce her. Love-crazed and desperate, he is soon moved to commit cynical acts of betrayal. And comic scenes involving a servant and his dog enhance the play's exploration of how passion can prove more powerful than even the strongest loyalty owed to a friend.

This book includes a general introduction to Shakespeare's life and the Elizabethan theatre, a separate introduction to *The Two Gentlemen of Verona*, a chronology of his works, suggestions for further reading, an essay discussing performance options on both stage and screen, and a commentary.

Edited by Norman Sanders

With an introduction by Russell Jackson

General Editor: Stanley Wells

PENGUIN SHAKESPEARE

THE WINTER'S TALE
WILLIAM SHAKESPEARE

WWW.PENGUINSHAKESPEARE.COM

The jealous King of Sicily becomes convinced that his wife is carrying the child of his best friend. Imprisoned and put on trial, the Queen collapses when the King refuses to accept the divine confirmation of her innocence. The child is abandoned to die on the coast of Bohemia. But when she is found and raised by a shepherd, it seems redemption may be possible.

This book includes a general introduction to Shakespeare's life and the Elizabethan theatre, a separate introduction to *The Winter's Tale*, a chronology of his works, suggestions for further reading, an essay discussing performance options on both stage and screen by Paul Edmondson, and a commentary.

Edited by Ernest Schanzer

With an introduction by Russ McDonald

General Editor: Stanley Wells

PENGUIN SHAKESPEARE

TIMON OF ATHENS
WILLIAM SHAKESPEARE

WWW.PENGUINSHAKESPEARE.COM

After squandering his wealth with prodigal generosity, a rich Athenian gentleman finds himself deep in debt. Unshaken by the prospect of bankruptcy, he is certain that the friends he has helped so often will come to his aid. But when they learn his wealth is gone, he quickly finds that their promises fall away to nothing in this tragic exploration of power, greed, and loyalty betrayed.

This book includes a general introduction to Shakespeare's life and the Elizabethan theatre, a separate introduction to *Timon of Athens*, a chronology of his works, suggestions for further reading, an essay discussing performance options on both stage and screen, and a commentary.

Edited by G. R. Hibbard

With an introduction by Nicholas Walton

General Editor: Stanley Wells

Read more in Penguin

PENGUIN SHAKESPEARE

All's Well That Ends Well
Antony and Cleopatra
As You Like It
The Comedy of Errors
Coriolanus
Cymbeline
Hamlet
Henry IV, Part I
Henry IV, Part II
Henry V
Henry VI, Part I
Henry VI, Part II
Henry VI, Part III
Henry VIII
Julius Caesar
King John
King Lear
Love's Labour's Lost
Macbeth
Measure for Measure
The Merchant of Venice
The Merry Wives of
    Windsor
A Midsummer Night's
    Dream
Much Ado About Nothing
Othello
Pericles
Richard II
Richard III
Romeo and Juliet
The Sonnets and A Lover's
    Complaint
The Taming of the Shrew
The Tempest
Timon of Athens
Titus Andronicus
Twelfth Night
The Two Gentlemen of
    Verona
The Two Noble Kinsmen
The Winter's Tale